THIS TO SHALL PASS

A Journey through Grief to the Other Side

Cathy Bamji

MOtivational PRESS®
LEADERS IN GLOBAL PUBLISHING

Published by Motivational Press, Inc.
1777 Aurora Road
Melbourne, Florida, 32935
www.MotivationalPress.com

Manufactured in the United States of America.

ISBN: 978-1-62865-410-3

CONTENTS

Portions of this book were previously printed in:

"Follow Your Instincts" previously appeared in
Heart By Heart: mothers and daughters listening to each other, iUniverse, 2004

"Grief Journey" previously appeared online at
www.quietmountainessays.com

"At My Center" previously appeared online at
www.quietmountainessays.com

IN MEMORIAM

※

JANICE W. GODFREY[1]
Simpsonville, SC

Janice W. Godfrey, 60, of 4 Bingham Way, died Saturday, May 1, 1999.

Born in Sewickley, PA, she was the daughter of the late John and Helen Kapron Wasilko. She spent her entire life with the single objective of being the best wife and mother, and she succeeded. She was a member of Disciples United Methodist Church.

She is survived by her husband, Thomas E. Godfrey, three daughters, Donna Godfrey Simpson of Raleigh, NC, Catherine Bamji of Silver Spring, MD and Tracy O'Ree of Mauldin, SC, and five grandchildren.

Services: 11:00 a.m. Tuesday at the Mackey Mortuary, Century Drive with Rev. Luone Rouse officiating. Burial will follow at Graceland East Memorial Park

Visitation: 7:00 until 8:30 p.m. Monday at The Mackey Mortuary Century Drive.

In lieu of flowers, memorials may be made to The Cancer Society of Greenville County, 113 Mills Ave., Greenville, SC 29605

---

1   This obituary appeared in The Greenville News, May 1999.

ACKNOWLEDGEMENTS

"How lucky I am to have something that makes saying goodbye so hard."

~ Winnie the Pooh

Encouragement for this book has come in many ways and from many people. I am blessed with loving friends and family who have supported my desire to provide a process of healing to others. Gratefully, there are too many to name, but I do wish to highlight a few people for their pivotal insights, understanding and guidance.

- To my mom, Jan Godfrey, whose daily guidance gives me the confidence and desire to make a difference and whose lessons taught me how to live and love.

- To my dad, Tom Godfrey, for his complete support and nagging demand that I do something with my writing.

- To my husband, Cyrus and our kids, for their unconditional love and acceptance and for providing me space in which to write and learn, cry and rejoice.

- To my friend and fellow writer, Carol Peck, whose idea it was to turn my personal writing into a guided journal for others to utilize.

- To my coach and friend, Eric Collier, who helped me realize how important it is to take things off the shelf.

FOREWORD

At some point, after a loss, some well-meaning person has told us *"That this too shall pass"*. The questions for many of us then are *"How will it pass?"* and *"Am I supposed to just hope time heals?"*

Losing a loved one presents us with a myriad of emotions that language never quite captures. In this book, Cathy provides a path for your heart to speak. She urges you to be fully human knowing you might have shared what you needed to say to your loved one, maybe not or maybe you said things you wish you could take back. Welcome to being human.

This Too Shall Pass isn't about simply waiting for time to pass, but rather to understand that the heart has expressions it must make to heal. To help us reconcile our feelings, Cathy reminds us that we are not alone. Grief is messy and isn't something to organize and succeed at. It's an exercise in allowing our hearts to say what needs to be said and feel what needs to be felt. In this book, Cathy offers us questions to reflect upon so we may begin to let go of what keeps us stuck and nourish the memories that feed our souls.

As a therapist and coach for over 25 years, I have had the privilege to support people along their path to healing from both the loss of a loved one and grief from unmet dreams. I am grateful to have *This Too Shall Pass* as a creative resource for my clients and I applaud your instinct to pick it up. I know you will be strengthened by reading, reflecting, and writing. You are on your path to healing.

Carolyn Spigel, LCSW- C, PCC

PREFACE

The common emotional stages of grief are those identified by Elisabeth Kübler-Ross in her 1969 book, *On Death and Dying*. They are: Denial, Anger, Bargaining, Depression and Acceptance. These stages are not meant to be a complete or final list of possible emotions nor are they necessarily experienced in a linear progression. Instead, they are offered as a foundation from which to understand what you *might* experience. Your path can be influenced by the type of loss, the kind of relationship, your age and health, physical proximity, etc. So, it should come as no surprise many of your experiences as well as my own have not followed these stages. Our experiences are all unique yet oddly similar. My personal journey began with my mother's diagnosis with lung cancer in 1996. I lived hundreds of miles away—in Maryland. She lived in South Carolina. The distance made things easier and more difficult. I walked gingerly (sometimes running, sometimes backtracking) on my path, winding my way through three years and four phases of grief.

My mother, Jan, developed lung cancer at the young age of 57 and passed at age 60. She was a loving wife, friend, mother and grandmother. She experienced many of these same stages of grief as she dealt with her own feelings, but one stage in particular was omitted—both from my mother's experience as well as my own. She never got angry. Her disposition set the stage for those around her. Her acceptance of her fate encouraged a sense of calmness and helped me move forward without anger or disappointment. Don't get me wrong, she did not simply give into the diagnosis, she fought the good fight. I am sure there were days when she was frustrated, but knowing her time was limited, she chose to spend it in joy and laughter, with family and friends. Today I live my life each day as fully as I can, taking advantage of every small moment and trying not to leave things unsaid. I welcome memories when they show up—then I cry a little, laugh a little and write; a process that will continue long after this book finds its way onto your shelf.

The pages of this book hold samples of my poems, essays and fragments, written during my own healing journey. I share these with the hope you can gain strength and confidence from the words and find light and comfort as you travel your own journey. Don't worry about your format, grammar or spelling, just let the words come in whatever shape they take. There *is* life after death—yours. Go forward, safe with the knowledge you can emerge happy and healthy and whatever you are feeling today it's okay. There is no judgment here, just blank pages and empty spaces for you to write notes, ask questions and record your memories. Let the words come and the healing begin. You might be surprised by what happens.

Phase 1: Realization

… awareness, understanding, apprehension…

Realization is the moment when you acknowledge the event, the trauma, the loss or potential loss. It begins with the initial communication and can last as long as it takes you to deal with the news. The actual amount of time is different for each of us.

"There is no despair so absolute as that which comes with the first moments of our first great sorrow, when we have not yet known what it is to have suffered and be healed, to have despaired and recovered hope."

- George Eliot

For me, it was a statement of fact. Mom had been to see multiple doctors concerned about a cough that just would not go away. They ran multiple tests all to the same answer: "Inconclusive." Until they weren't and mom was finally diagnosed with lung cancer. By the time the doctors were able to determine this fact, the cancer had spread. Surgery was not an option and she was given six months. The doctors recommended she "get her house in order" to which my mom replied, "I don't have time to die. I have grandchildren to raise." Mom had set the stage. She was not exactly in denial, but she was not accepting her fate as the final word either. She simply acknowledged the facts as she saw them and moved forward from there. And so did the rest of us.

I recognize my mom was an exception to the rule—having not experienced Denial and Anger in the usual manner. Reality is that most people (both those who are ill and their caregivers) do progress through an Anger stage; a stage where they are lost and seek understanding. It will do little for me to tell you not to be angry, but channel that anger, understand the fear which drives it, spend time seeing it for what it is, then let it go.

What is your situation? What are you holding on to?

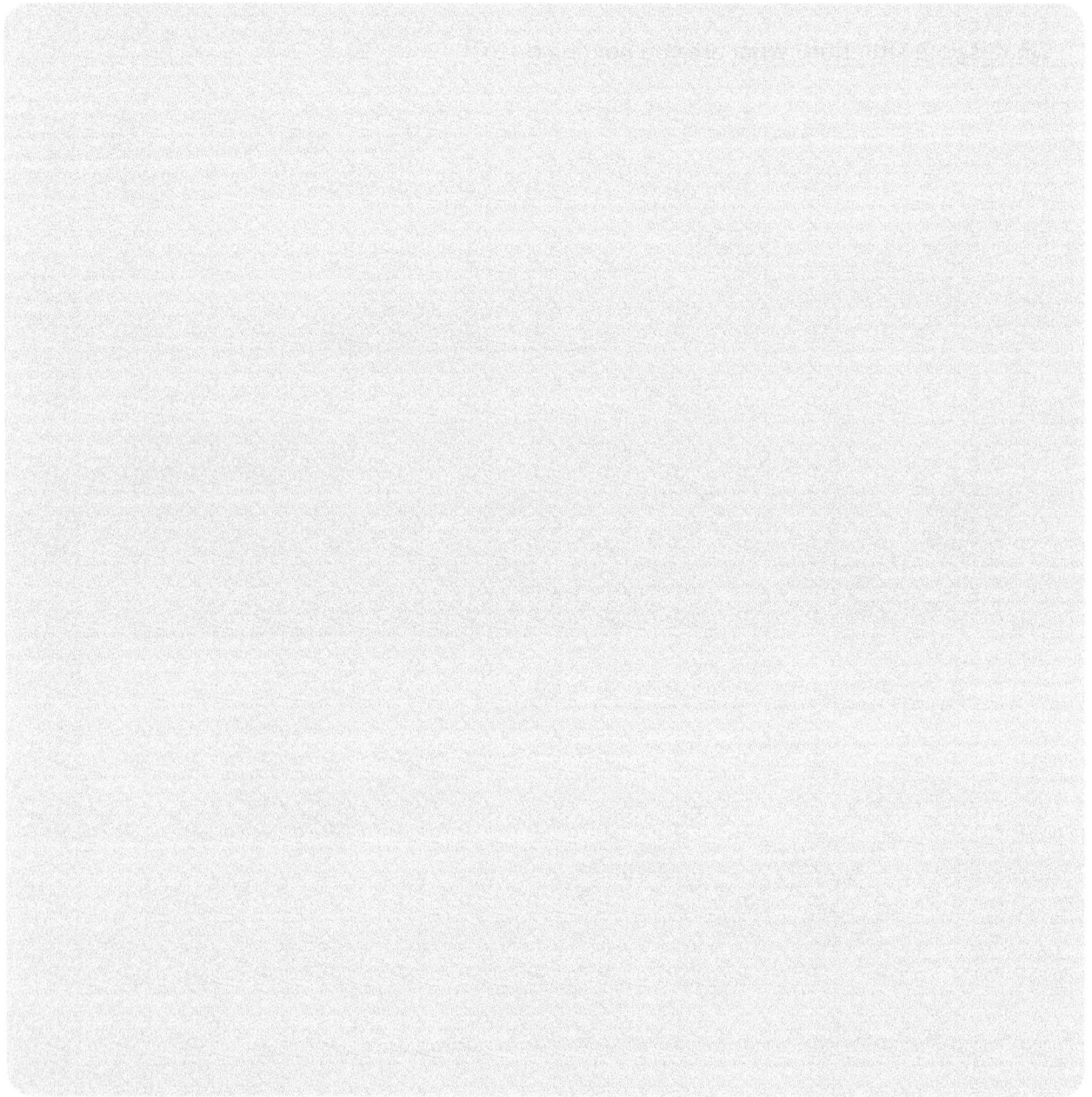

Phase 1: Realization

CALLING HOME

There was always one more question to ask, one more issue to discuss, one more achievement to convey. When I called home mom was always happy to listen, pleased to advise, proud to hear all my news. She laughed and told me what I needed to hear. She sounded just as she always had, filling my mind with information and warnings of what might happen next. She couldn't help but remind me of my own childhood antics and that history repeats itself. I easily forgot she was sick, that she must sit down to speak with me because to walk about required too much oxygen. It didn't occur to me she struggled before answering the phone, preparing her body and voice. She worked hard not to show signs of illness. She didn't complain. She didn't whine. She didn't even talk about how the medicine was making her feel. She was just my mom, answering my questions, laughing at my kids and enjoying life.

I called, not out of obligation or concern. I called, selfishly, because she was my mother and she had the answers. That is what being a mother is. That was her role for me. What I expect and wanted and needed. But then I would take a trip home with my two little boys in tow. She did not reach down to lift them up. She could not run after them, catch them and throw them in the air. The only way they could interact with her was to sit with her in the big armchair in the den or at the kitchen table. But they didn't seem to mind. They didn't know the difference. Weren't all grandmothers meant to be sat upon and crawled over? But, I knew. I knew the difference between the kind of mother she was and the kind of grandmother she had to be. And I felt guilty for my trivial phone calls.

I returned home and the calls began again. I couldn't help myself. She was too much a part of my daily life. There were too many questions I couldn't answer, too many stories to tell. But she said she didn't mind. She said my questions kept her mind active, her memories flowing. She said this was the life she had and the one she would continue, until she didn't.

Take a moment for yourself - pause, breathe deeply and allow yourself to let go of all judgment, fear and anger. With self-compassion and thoughtfulness, write down what's in your head - and in your heart.

What do you wish for, long for? What do you want to say or never had the chance to say?

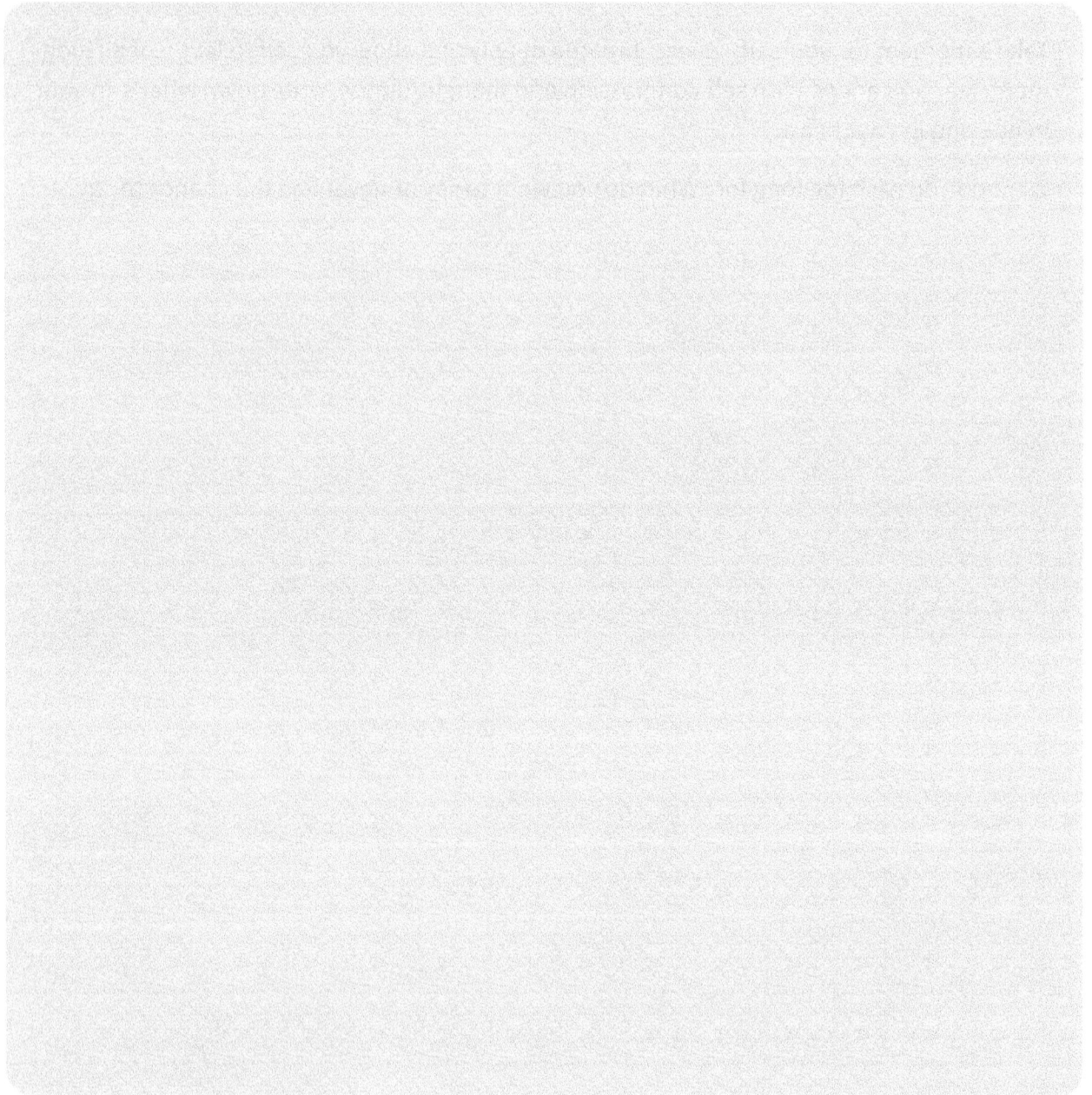

NOTE TO MOM

"What's that smell? Don't you smell it?"

How many times I heard you say that.

I hope I never discover what it was.

Hope I never smell it myself.

"The fears we don't face become our limits."

- Robin Sharma

Fear is not uncommon at this point. Take the time to acknowledge and understand your fears. What are you afraid of?

Give voice to your fears, say them out loud, write them down, share them with another; acknowledging how you feel may provide opportunities for discovery and comfort .

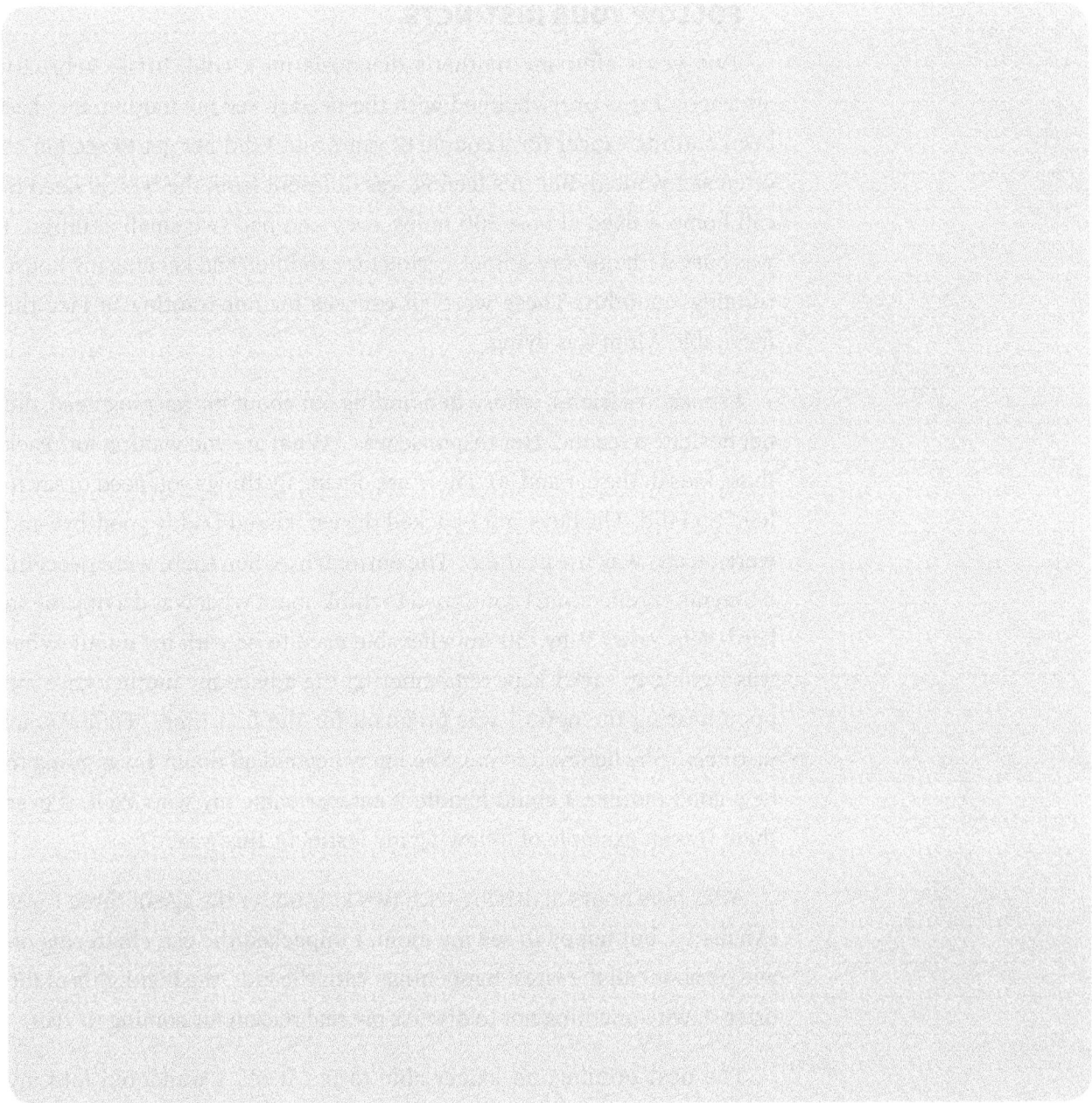

FOLLOW YOUR INSTINCTS

Two years after my mother's diagnosis on a cold, brisk, February afternoon I was overwhelmed with the need to see my mother. She had been battling cancer for a couple of years and I did not get to see her as often as I wanted. But this feeling was different from the typical need to call home. I lived almost 500 miles away and had two small children. I was busy with nursery school, caring for a toddler, and keeping my house running smoothly. These were all excuses for not wanting to face the inevitable. Mom was dying.

I spoke to a friend, who, when finding out about my nagging need, did not hesitate a second. Her response was, "What are you waiting for! Pack those kids in the car and go. There are obviously things you need to say to her." So I did. The boys and I packed the car, kissed Daddy good-bye and were on our way the next day. The entire trip, when there were peaceful moments of reflection, I continued to think about what was driving me so hard. Why now? Why this unbelievable need to be with my mom? What was I going to say? I kept remembering the advice my mother gave me upon hearing the news I was pregnant for the first time: "Follow your instincts." She believed in me. She knew beyond all doubt I was going to be a good mother, I could handle whatever came my way. Well, if ever there was an example of following my instincts, this was it.

After nine hours of driving with two kids under the age of three I was exhausted, but happy to see my mom. I unpacked the car, chattering on and on about all the latest happenings with the kids, the highlights of the drive down—anything not to discuss my real reason for coming to visit.

The next evening, no longer able to put it off, I wandered into my mom's bedroom, as I had done so many times before. There she was, sitting in bed, reading glasses on her face, covers pulled to her waist. I can feel the softness of her sheets and the warmth of her heart. I began to cry as I do now. She looked at me and asked what was wrong. I opened my mouth still unsure what was going to come out and said, "Thank you. Thank you for teaching me how to live, for being patient, for being there whenever I needed you, for teaching me how to be a mother, without judging me. Thanks for loving me even when it was difficult, when I lied to you, when I said I hated you. Thanks for teaching me how to love a man for who he is and accepting people, trusting people and facing the world head on. Astonishingly enough you have not only taught me all these things, you have now taught me how to die."

During the course of her illness, my mom never once uttered the words "why me?" never once cried or complained as the toxic liquid filled her veins. She faced each treatment, each stack of pills, each new food, the nausea, the pain, the lack of oxygen, with complete acceptance. This was her fate, her destiny, perhaps her reason for living. She was teaching others, teaching me, how to live a good life and to die fighting, proud of who we are, the life we lived, the lives we created.

"There is a voice that doesn't use words... Listen!"
-Rumi

Find a quiet place. Give yourself permission to relax your body and quiet your mind. What do you hear?

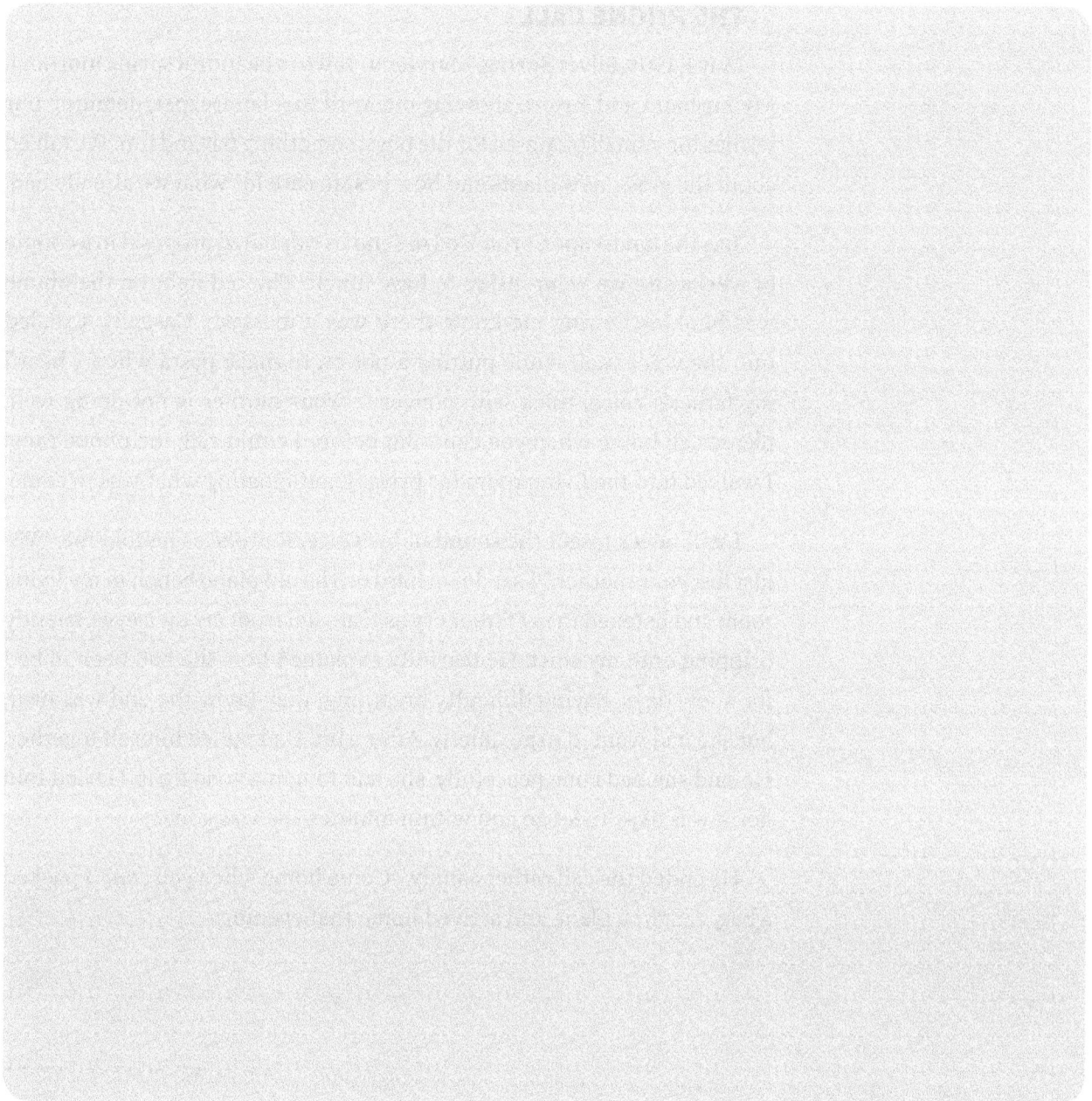

THE PHONE CALL

May 1, 1999, Silver Spring, Maryland. It was a beautiful spring morning. My husband and I were showing our yard to a landscaper, detailing our wishes for a small play area for the boys, something flat and fun. We talked about the grass, new plants and how best to care for what we already had.

Joe, the landscaper, promised to send us a detailed proposal in a couple of weeks and we went inside to have lunch. The red light on the phone was blinking, letting me know there was a message. Casually, I dialed into the voice mail while putting a pot on to make pasta when I heard my father's voice, thick with concern, "Your mother is not doing well, please call home when you can." But before I could call, the phone rang. I walked into the living room for privacy, anticipating what was to come.

I will never forget the sound of his voice, it broke as he told me, "We just lost your mother." I sat down hard on the old piano bench in my living room and listened to my father cry as tears fell from my own eyes, silently dripping onto my shirt. He tearfully explained how she had been in bed for a few days, having difficulty breathing; they knew the end was near, but she had wanted to go quietly. After a bit, Dad pulled himself together. He said she had gone peacefully, she had fought a good fight. He had told her it was okay to let go and within minutes she was gone.

He ended the call rather calmly, "Come home when you can." I packed a bag, caught a plane and arrived home that evening.

There's a moment when reality hits you and things will never be the same. What was your moment? What were you feeling? What were thinking?

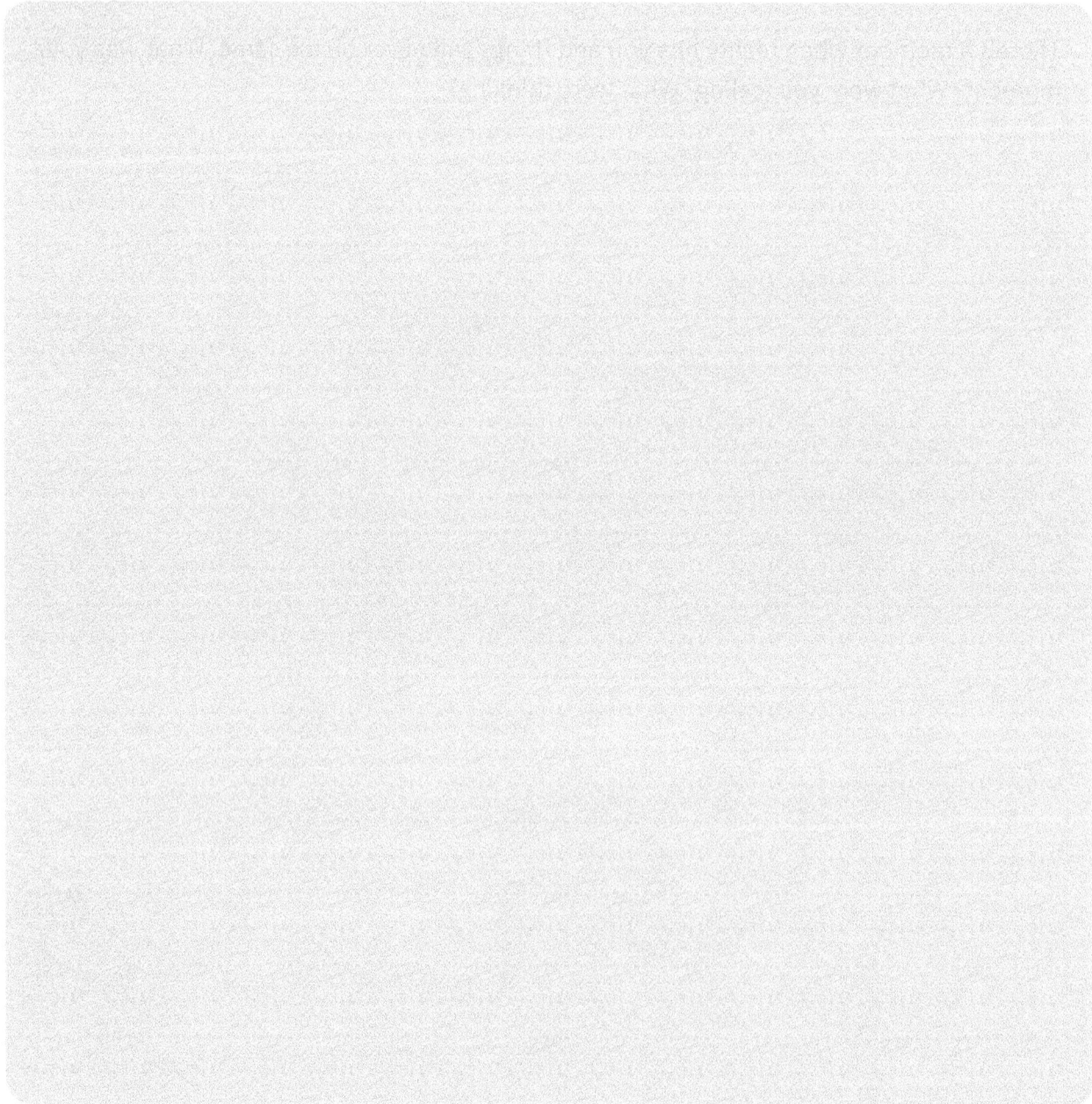

GOOD-BYE[2]

May 1, 1999

Dear Mom,

It is my belief your soul continues, making the world a better place. I wanted to see you again before you left, but it wasn't meant to be.

Thanks for your unending dedication and love—your advice, your example. I pray my boys will respect and love me as much as I love you.

My tears are selfish; I realize there are many things I would like to have had happen, mostly to have my boys really know you. Your physical presence will be missed, but you will exist in our hearts and through our actions. Your spiritual presence will remain in this world as powerful positive energy; in this knowledge I find comfort.

I'll miss your warmth, your smell, your voice. I'll miss knowing you are only a phone call away. I'll miss your hugs and everything about you.

Love you.

> *" [P]eople will forget what you said, people will forget what you did, but people will never forget how you made them feel."*
>
> *~ Maya Angelou*

---

2   Written on the plane en route home the day my mom passed.

What final words do you have? Write a letter to your loved one. Take the time to say all the things you need to say—what you are grateful for, how they made you feel, what you will remember most, the lessons and the laughter.

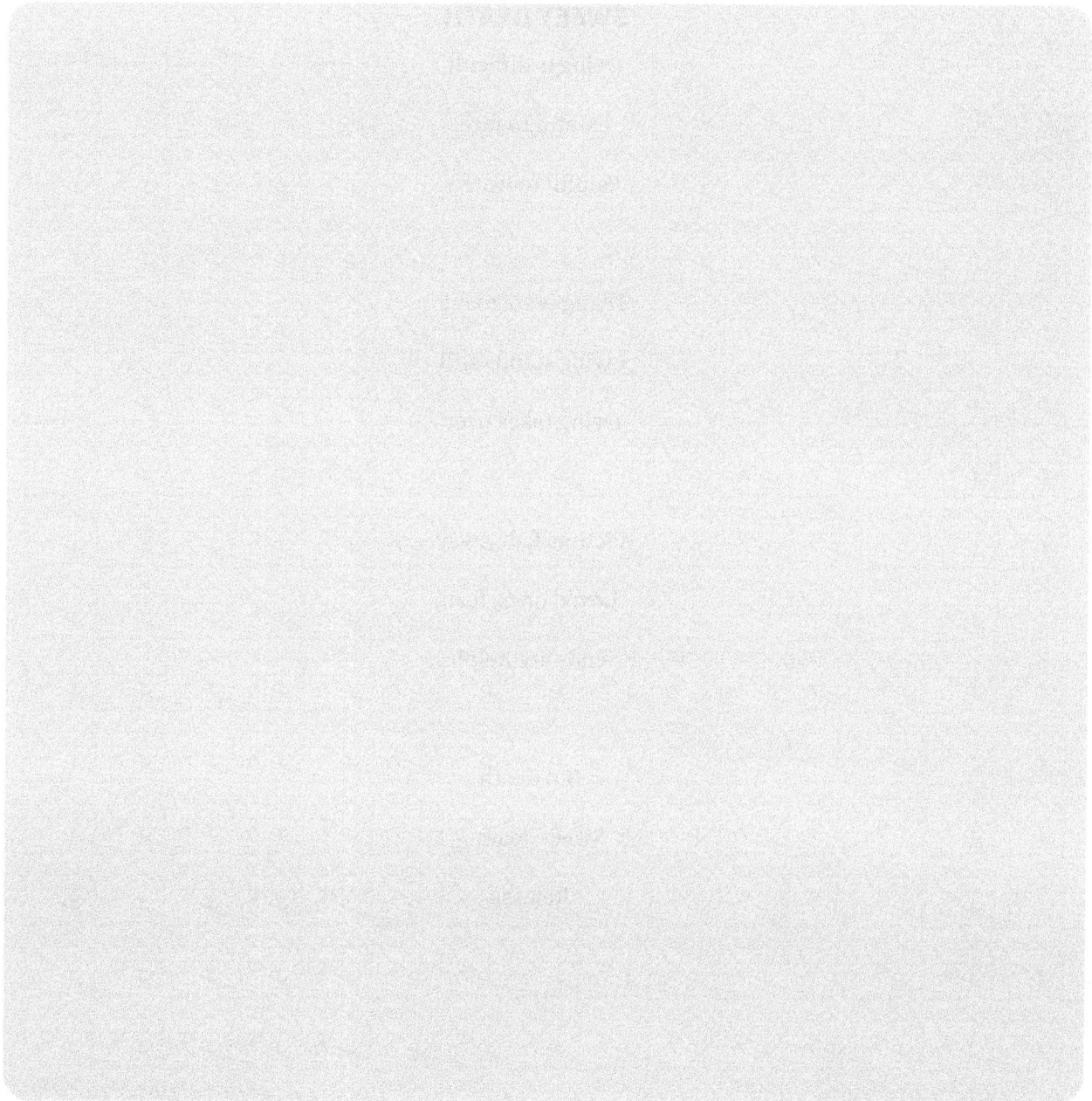

SWEET DEATH

Dying is difficult

Painful to face

Painful to watch

Dying is stagnant

Living stands still

Dying takes over

Victims fade away

Loved ones, fear

Friends are helpless

But death

Sweet death—

Release

Resist judging yourself - there's no right or wrong. Just write down phrases and words that come to mind when you think about your loss.

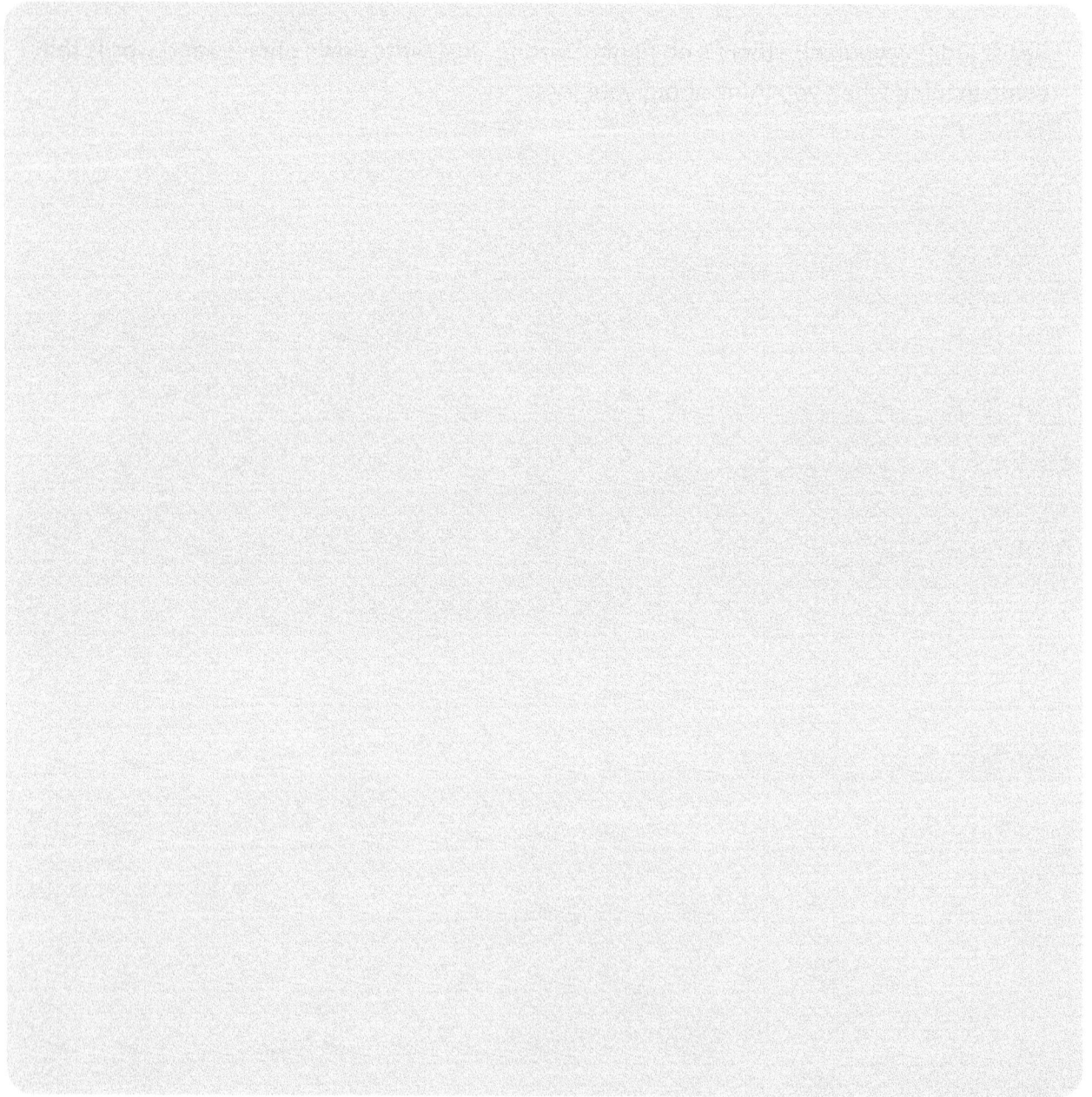

WHY GO, YOU'RE NOT THERE...

It's a cold, indifferent place

Mounds of dirt, flowers and stone

Six feet under

A long box sits; a body lies still, dressed and blessed

Flattened ground and marker clear

Place of focus or sadness or fear

Why would I go ... you're not there

All of us grieve in different ways. No single way is right or wrong. During the funeral my older sister held her tears and delivered mom's eulogy. It was beautiful and moving. She mourned privately, preferring to keep her grief private. My younger sister finds comfort in visiting mom's grave. It brings her closer; there she is better able to speak with mom without observation, without judgment. I prefer to write—it brings me clarity and provides an outlet for my conflicting feelings.

How do you grieve? What is your release?

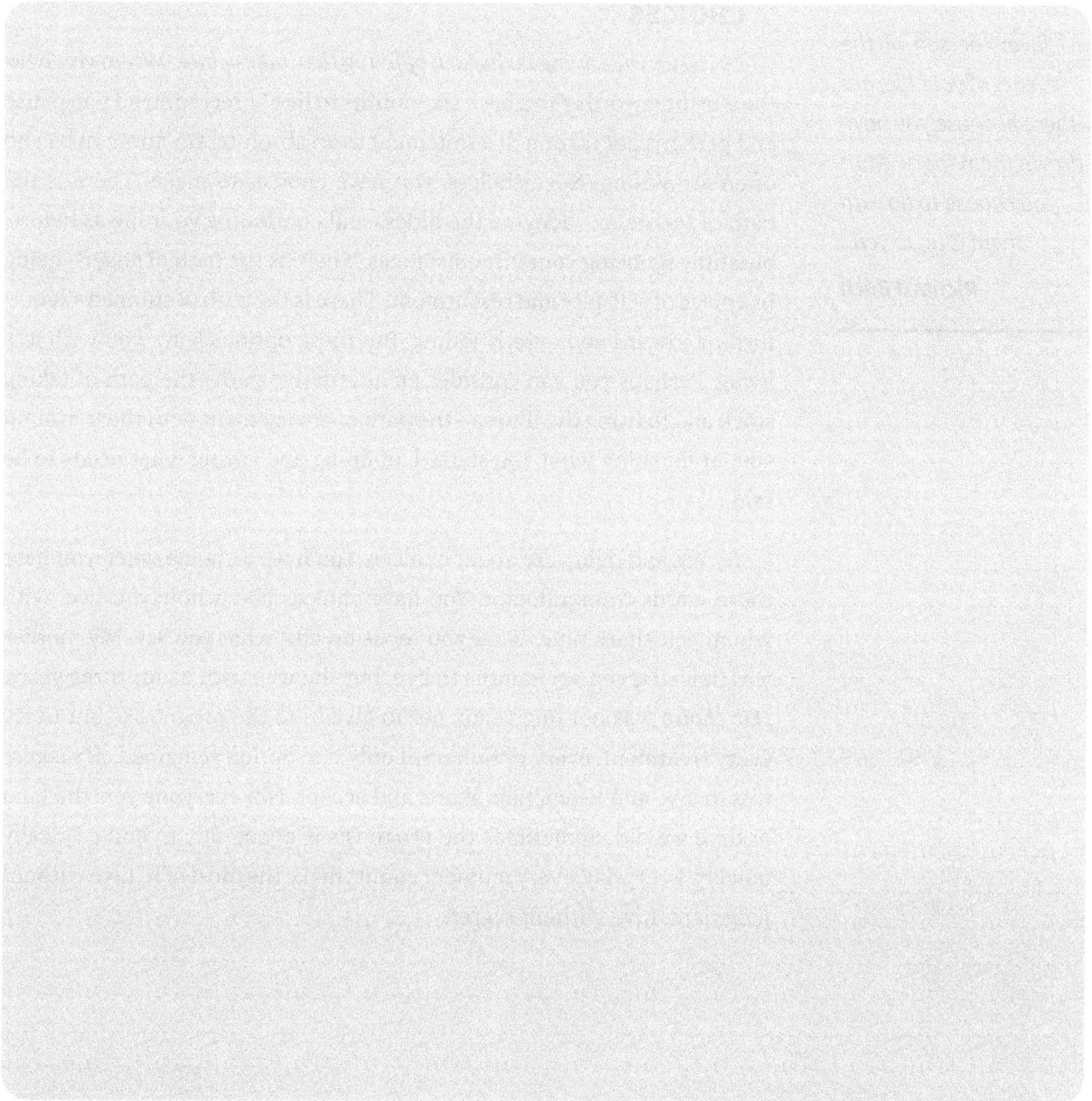

> *"Every person, all the events of your life, are there because you have drawn them there. What you choose to do with them is up to you."*
>
> **-Richard Bach**

CHOICES

My issue with dying is the lack of living that takes place. When you hear the startling words "You have six months to live" I recommend you pause and perhaps not take such a statement as an absolute. Doctors can be and often are wrong. Nevertheless, you have choices to make. There is the path of resistance: denying the illness and continuing your life as before, blissfully ignoring your circumstances. There is the path of anger—living in a place of self-pity and resentment. There is the path of stunned silence: turning inward and quietly fading. But these options leave you with less *living*. Perhaps you can consider an alternative path—the path of taking stock and fighting the illness—the path of engagement with those around you, of finishing what you started, of doing and saying what needs to be said.

Living and dying are about choices. You have a choice when you hear those words from a doctor. You have choices about how you live, with whom you share time, what you focus on and what you say. My mother was indeed given six months to live, but she was with us for three years. *Her choice* was not to give up, not to give in to the prognosis—but to try every treatment, every option until only one option remained. *My choice* was to love and listen, talk, share, and accept. Not everyone gets the kind of time we did. Sometimes the prognosis is good, only to end tragically quickly. Every day, every moment counts make the most of it. Live without judgment. Live without regret.

We cannot choose our feelings. We can only choose our response. What were your reactions? What did you learn about yourself?

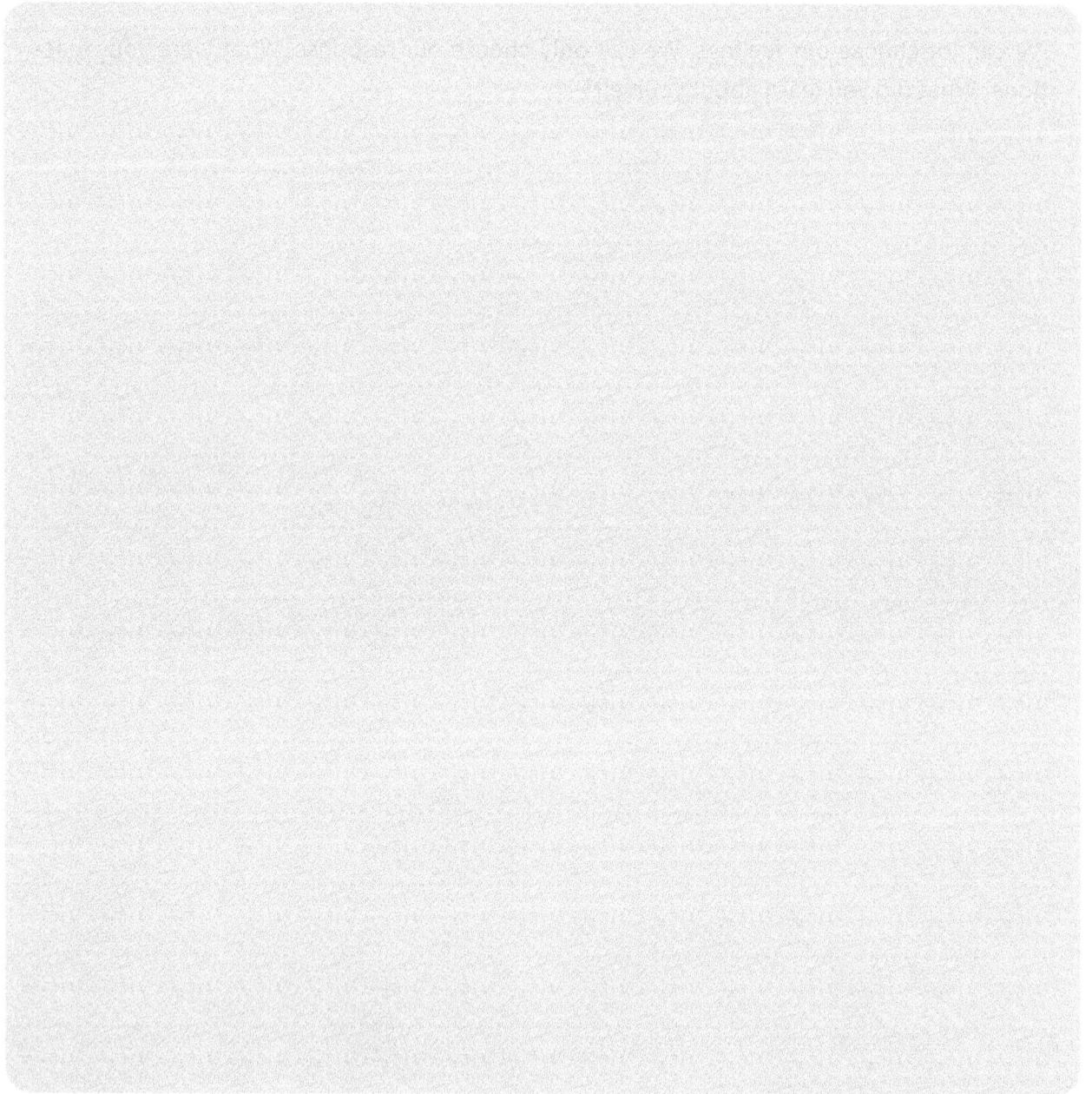

WHERE LIFE IS LIVED

Dying ...

Is painful and difficult

The victim is slow and labored

The caregiver, sad and on edge

Each moment holds silent thoughts

What could have been

What should have been

Whys and why nots

Each day filled with questions and worry

Pills to take, doctors to see—

Waiting and longing.

Each week offers hope, unfulfilled

Provides opportunities, untaken

Death...

Has finality,

It's finished

Done

"The purpose of life is to live it, to taste experience to the utmost, to reach out eagerly and without fear for newer and richer experience."

~ Eleanor Roosevelt

The victim moves on

The caregiver stops

Moments stand still

Blurring present with past

The waiting is done

The longing, deeper

All hope, discontinued

It is in the release

The change

The shift

Where life is lived

Where time ticks forward

Longing to rest

Grief to opportunity

Sadness to promise

Take a moment to reflect on how your life has changed. Be honest with yourself and allow your thoughts freedom of expression.

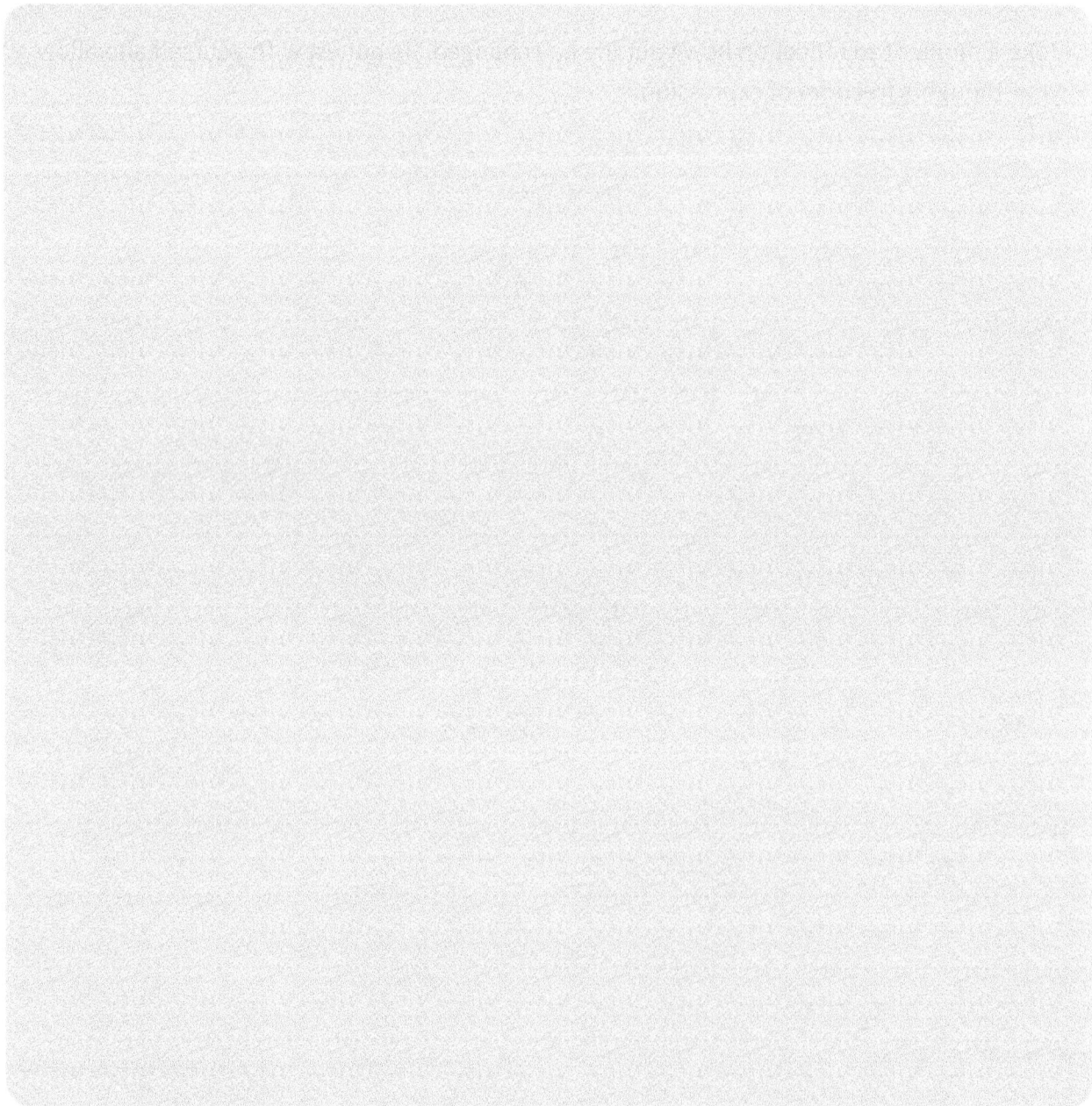

Phase 2: Depression

... hopelessness, sadness, melancholy...

When you are close to someone you can't help but feel sad when they pass. Even if great suffering was not involved, death is still sad; you may feel a bit lost and alone, even with friends and family around. There will be mini-episodes of picking up the phone to share a funny story—you might even dial the number only to realize while the pre-recorded message answers in your ear that your loved one is no longer available. It is that void, that absence where sadness engulfs you.

"In the midst of winter, I found there was, within me, an invincible summer."

- Albert Camus

Periods of sadness are normal and to be expected. But if you find it is interfering with your functioning and you are unable to complete daily activities then you might consider reaching out to someone who can help you navigate your feelings of sadness and depression. Seek out a counselor: someone you can trust and feel comfortable with, someone who empowers you and helps you to resolve your sadness. You may not find this person on your first phone call or meeting, but find him or her you will. Honor of your sadness—listen to it, give voice to it, write down its stories.

Grief can result in bouts of sadness, emptiness and loneliness. Allow yourself to express these feelings here.

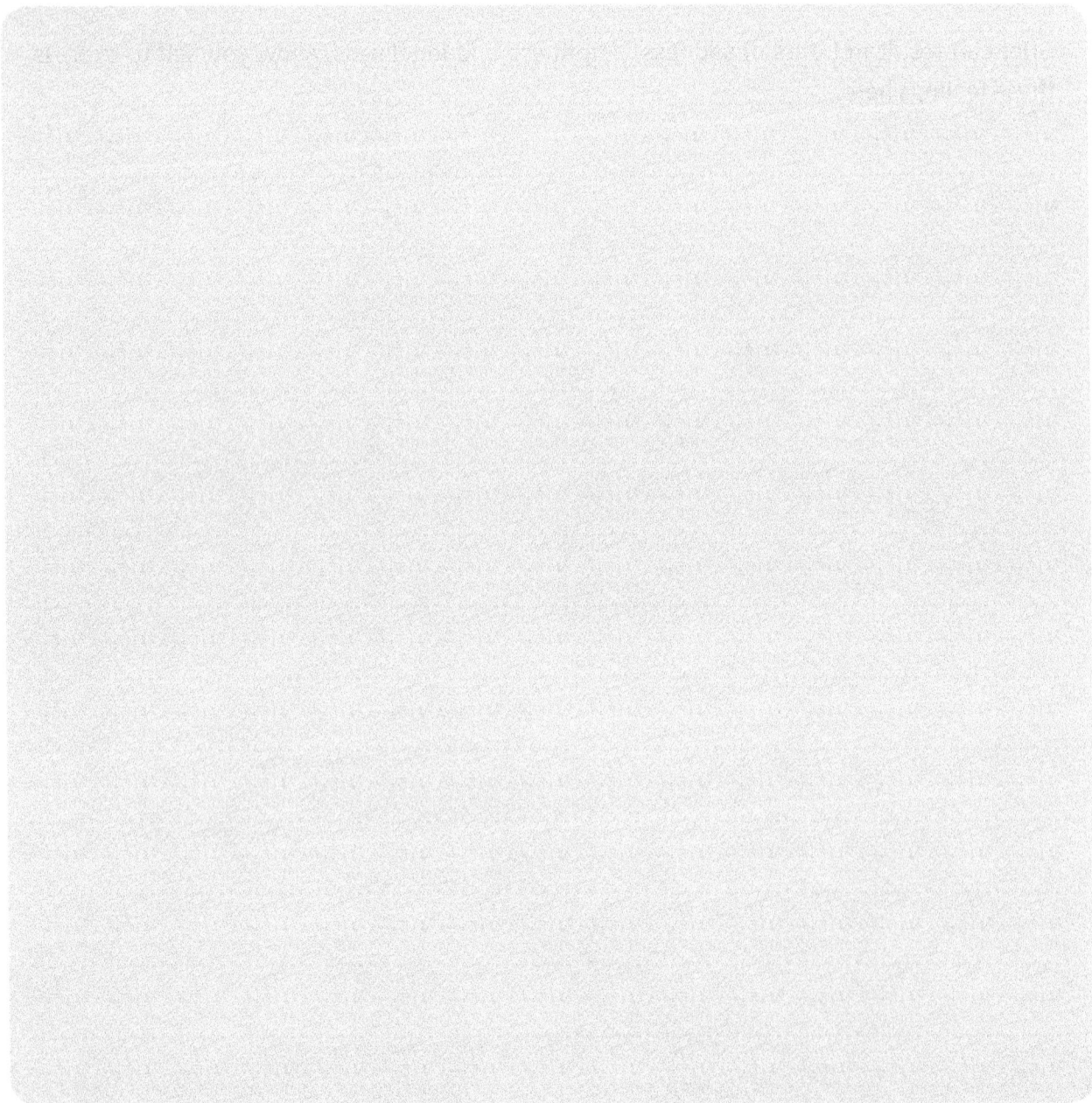

THIS TOO SHALL PASS

I never missed you more than I missed you today. It was raining, kids in the house all day—loud, rude, noisy, laughing, disobedient, mean and funny. One moment I found myself screaming to be heard, banging my hands on the toy train table, and the next I was collapsing to the floor in disgust and relief; hugging and soothing my four-year-old, apologizing and asking forgiveness for losing control, again.

I rode the wave up and down three more times before collapsing on the couch with a whiskey and a bowl of ice cream.

How did you do it? How I wish you were here to tell me your secrets, or at least hold me again and tell me once more "This too shall pass."

"When you get to the end of your rope, tie a knot and hang on."

~ Franklin Delano Roosevelt

What are you in need of today?

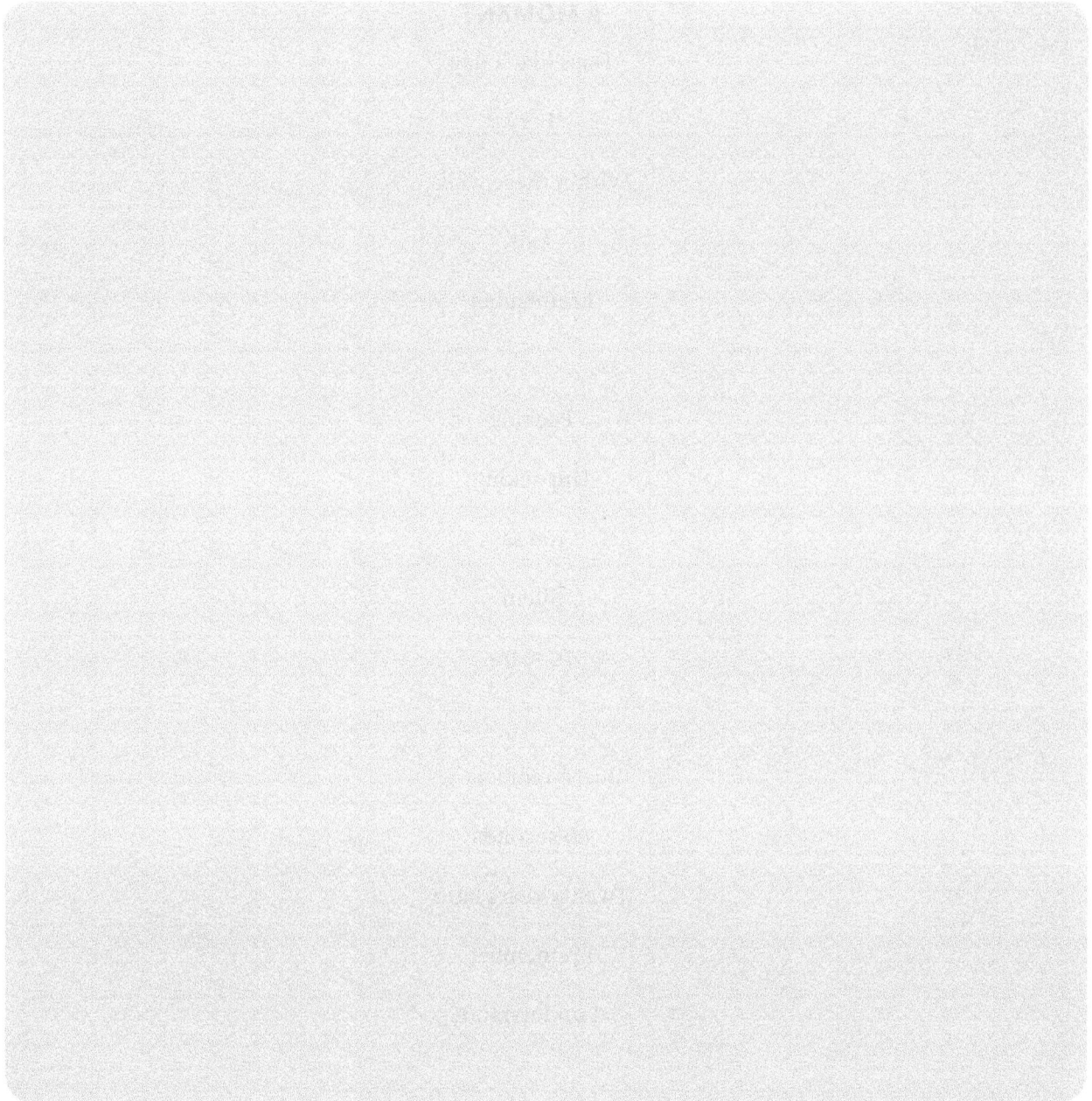

A MOMENT

Days like today

I cry

Within these walls

I sit

I remember

Packing

Unpacking

You sat

Silent

In tears

Just a moment –

60 seconds

Twenty years later

I remember

I understand

Grief can also result in feelings of fear, desperation and anger. Releasing these feelings helps us begin to let go.

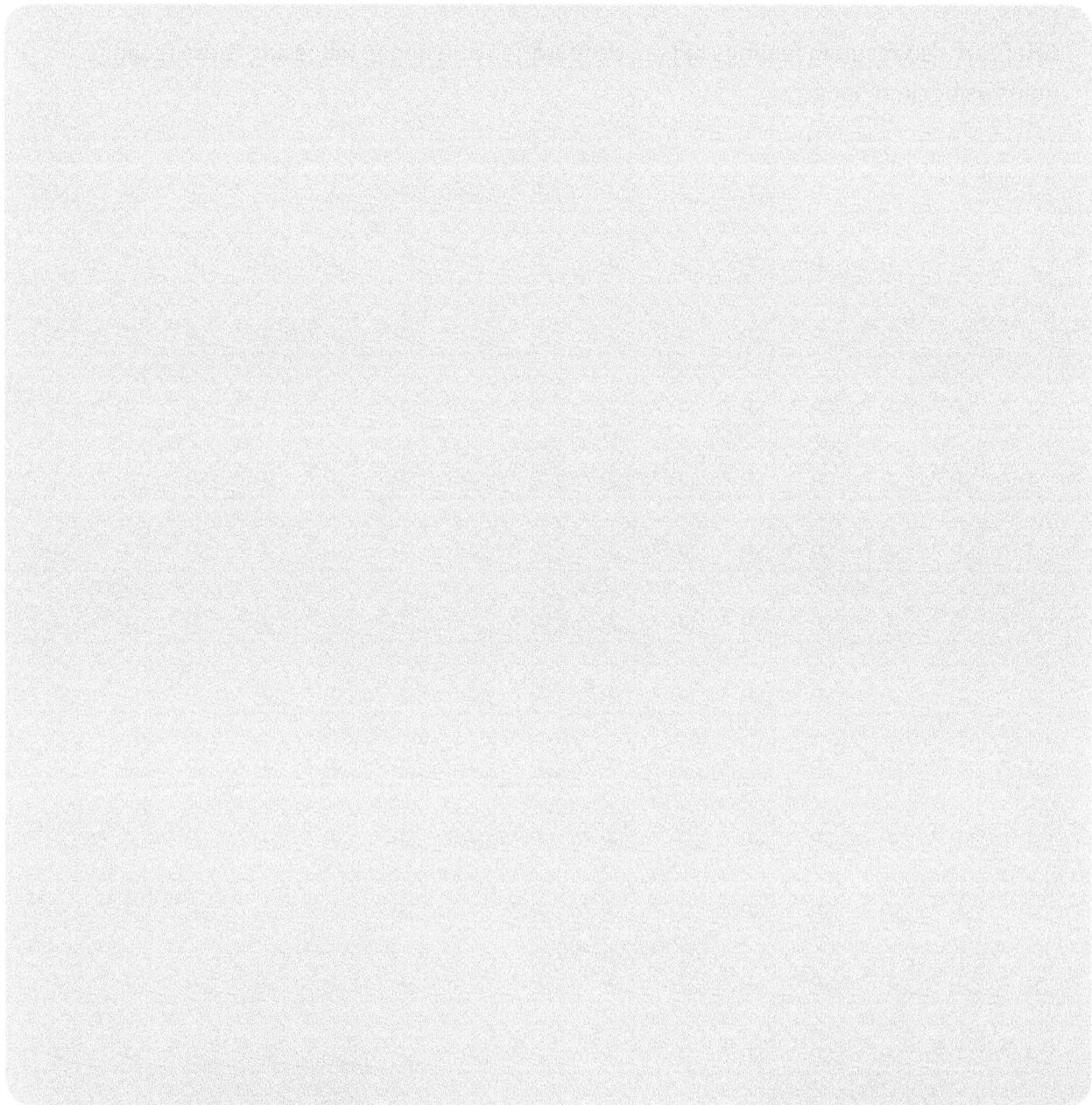

KNOWING IS NOT ENOUGH

Dear God:

Mom never said it and I don't remember having said it until now… now I want to know. Why? Why *my* mom? Why should her light go out so early? She was only 60. I look around this café and can't help listening to the older women behind me, talking about all their old friends, 70's, 80's, 90's. My mom was so young. What made her so different from these women?

I'm not angry, really I'm not. I understand intellectually all life ends, it was her time, she had completed her task. I know she lives on in me, in my sisters, in her grandchildren. I know my father won't let her memory be forgotten. But, I want to talk to her, lay across her bed at night and tell her about my day, about all the silly things my kids did and said.

I know she's with me, but there are times when I want to hold her and be held by her. I want to smell her familiar scent and bathe in her love. I want to ask my questions. I want to be given the answers. I'm tired of doing this without her.

Help.

"We want lives of simple, predictable ease—smooth, even trails as far as the eye can see—but God likes to go off-road. He provokes us with twists and turns. He places us in predicaments that seem to defy our endurance and comprehension—and yet don't. By his love and grace, we persevere."

*~ **Tony Snow***

What path lies ahead? Where is the universe leading you today? Take some time, reflect and write.

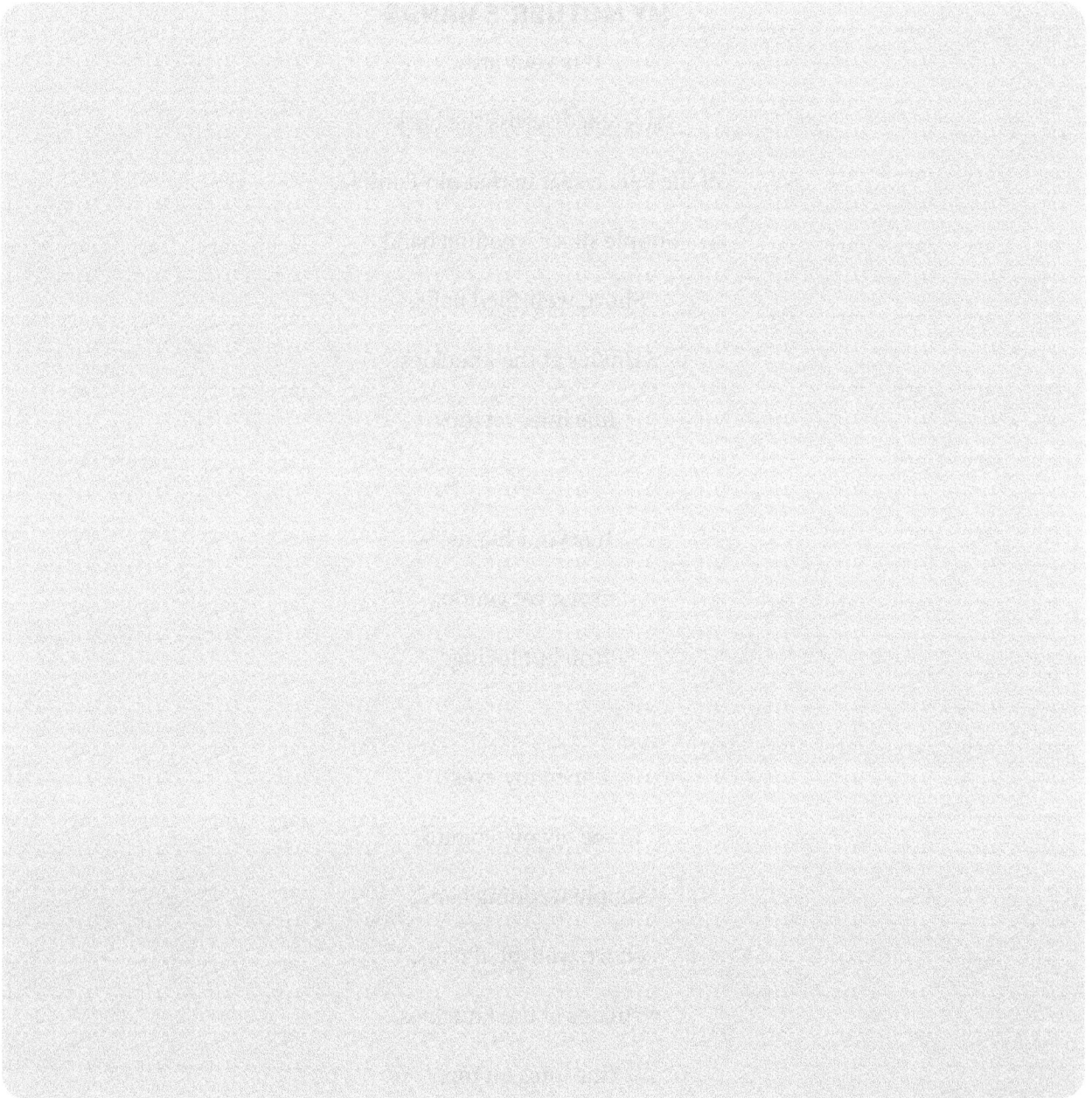

MY MOTHER'S HANDS

It is your arm,

stretched across the back

of the bench seat in that old Pontiac.

Simple silver wedding band,

Short, well-filed nails,

wrinkles at the knuckles,

fine lines on top.

It is your hands,

strong yet gentle,

firm but loving.

I open my eyes,

to see my own hands,

simple wedding band,

short, well-filed nails,

wrinkles at the knuckles,

fine lines on top.

I reach for my boys and

pray my hands are as

strong, gentle, firm and loving

as those that held me

so many years ago.

"Only if you have been in the deepest valley can you know how magnificent it is to be on the highest mountain."

~ Richard Milhous Nixon

As you travel through your grief towards healing, draw a picture describing how you feel today and where you want to go.

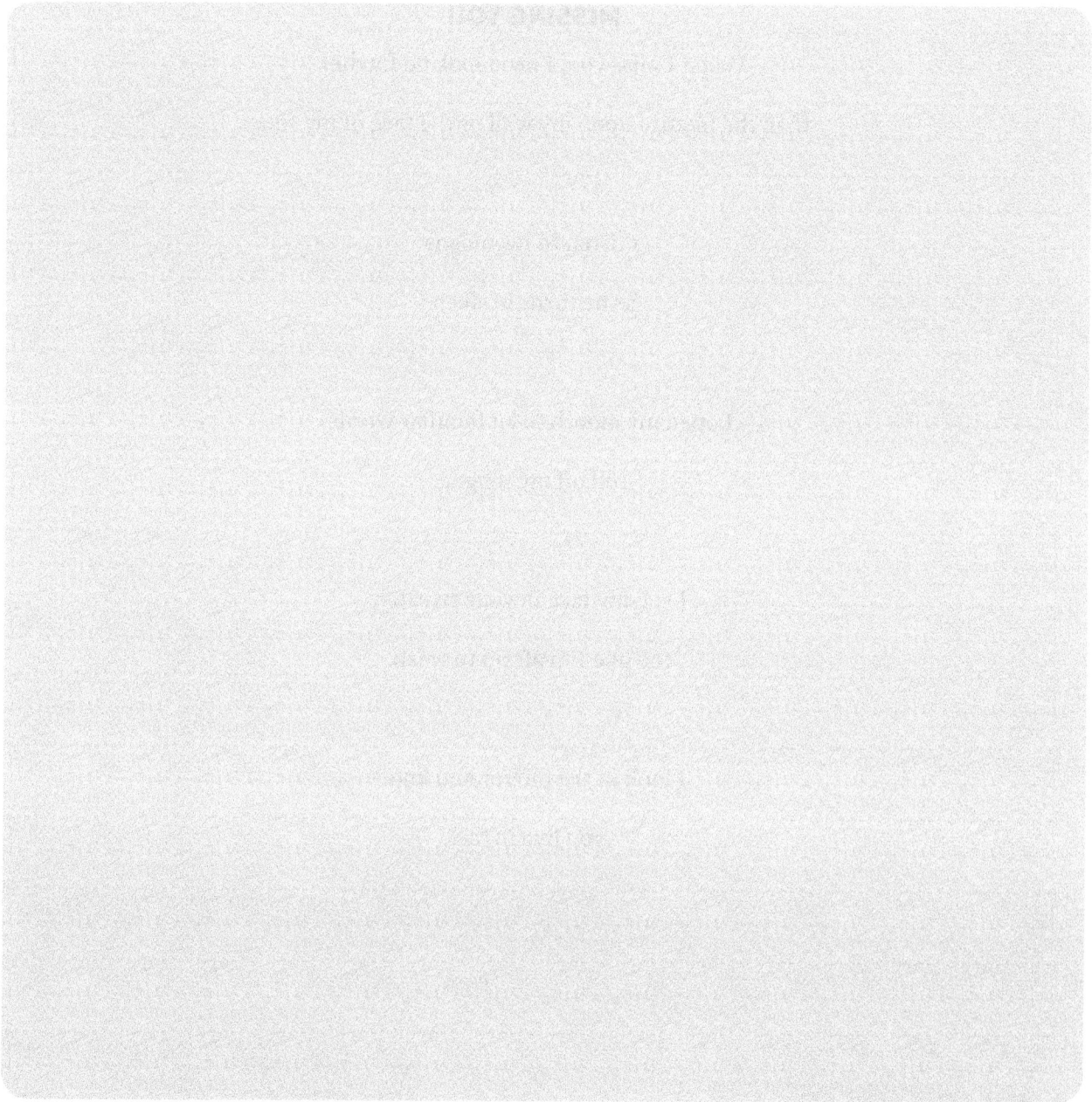

MISSING YOU

When I miss you, I need look no further

than the picture upon my wall or the face of my son.

I listen to his moans

as he turns in sleep.

I open my mouth to let familiar words

roll off my tongue.

I rub my face in your sweater,

the one I'm afraid to wash.

I look in the mirror and know

you live in me.

It is okay to miss your loved one and it is okay to want to move on. Resist punishing yourself with regret and guilt. Take this opportunity to write down those things left unspoken—what do you wish you had said, not said, done or not done?

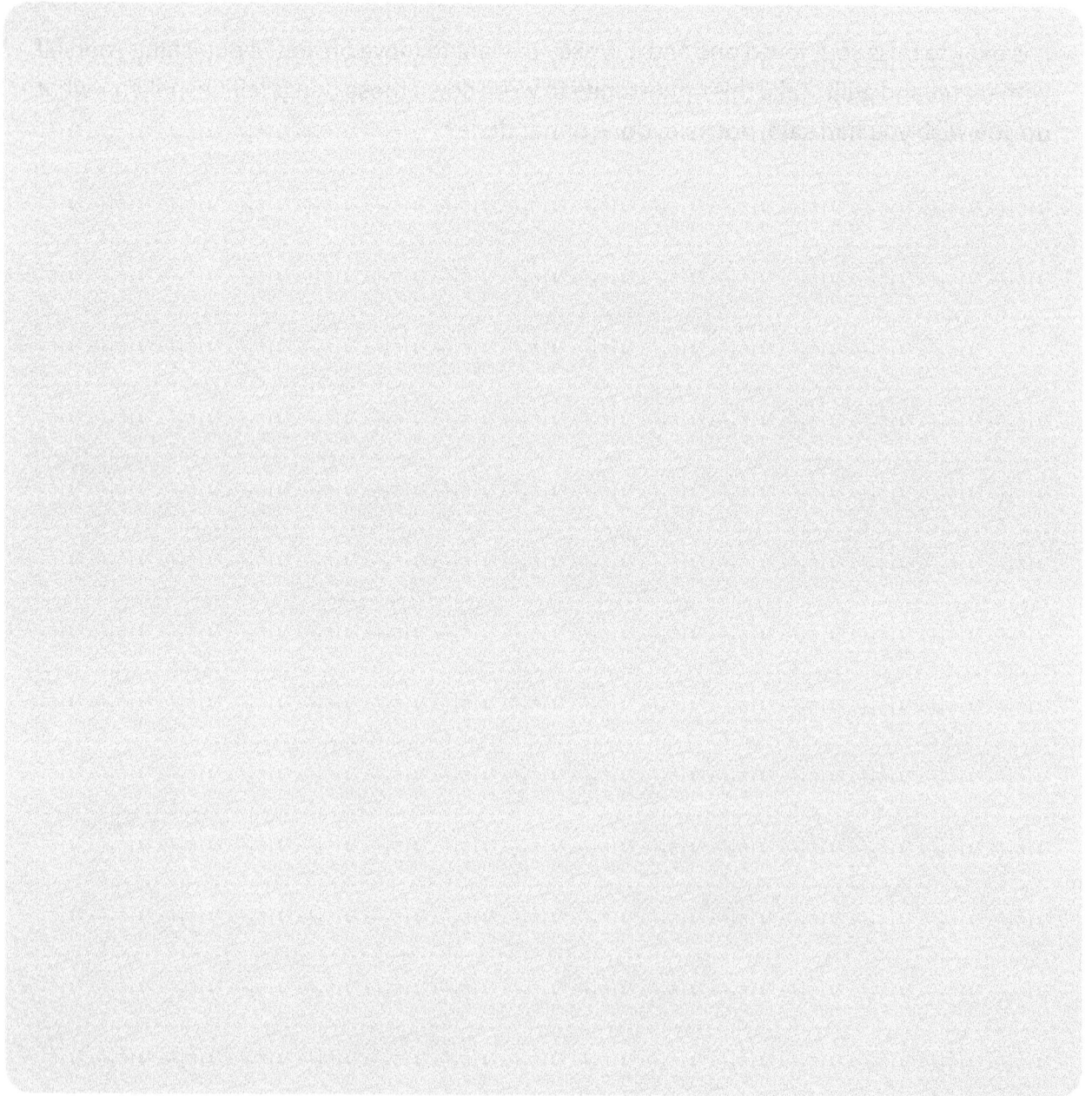

THERE'S A HOLE IN MY HEART

There's a hole in my heart

Where you used to be.

As time has passed

There has been no one to fill it,

No one to hug,

No one to laugh with, cry with,

Make love with.

There's a hole in my heart

Where your love was.

Deep within my soul,

I feel the pain of loss

Growing, feeding off me

Killing me slowly, day by day—

Emptying my being.

There's a hole in my heart

Where mending must take place;

For I am alive, with children

And grandchildren to love;

With new dreams to be created and

New loves to be discovered.

NOTE: During my sadness over losing my mom I was also worried about my dad. Putting myself in his place and imaging how it would feel to lose my spouse, I wrote this poem. It was an uplifting experience for me and helped me express my wish for him to move forward.

Imagine someone who cares deeply about you and wants the best for you. What are they telling you? What do they wish for you? What do they hope you will understand?

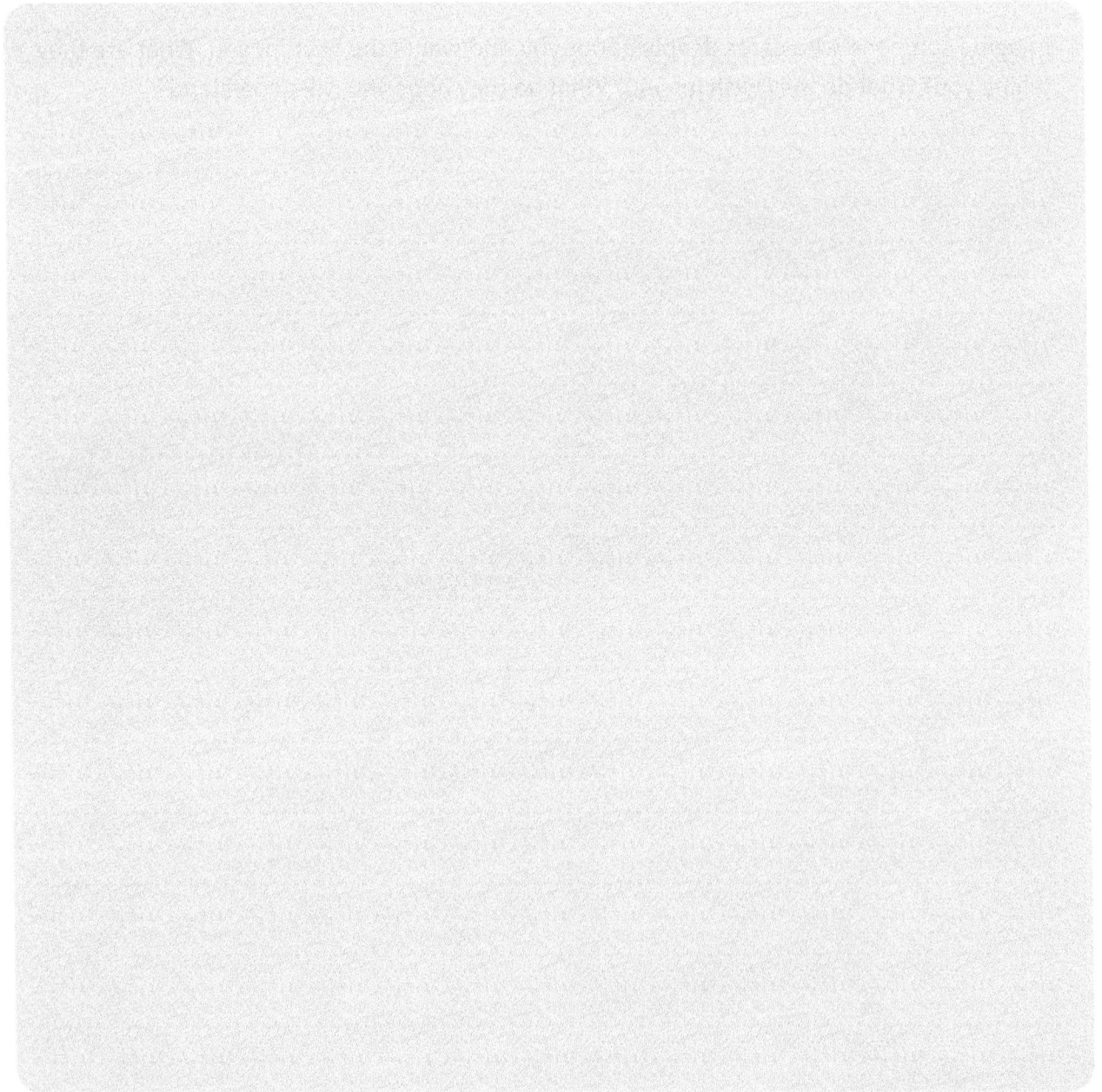

Phase 3: Acceptance

❧ ✦ ☙

… recognition, acknowledgment, understanding …

Acceptance is a turning point –

…moments in time where the subconscious mind works hard to process what the conscious mind cannot handle. For most of us these moments take place in dreams—both at night while you sleep and during the day through daydreams, visions, prayers and memories. There you can discover important lessons, find guidance and, ultimately, a sense of calm.

Acceptance is the pivot from death to living—the cross street between standing still and moving forward. It will happen; it has to happen. It is the path to healing.

"What the caterpillar calls the end of the world, the master calls a butterfly."

- Richard Bach

What are you feeling now? What do you need to move forward?

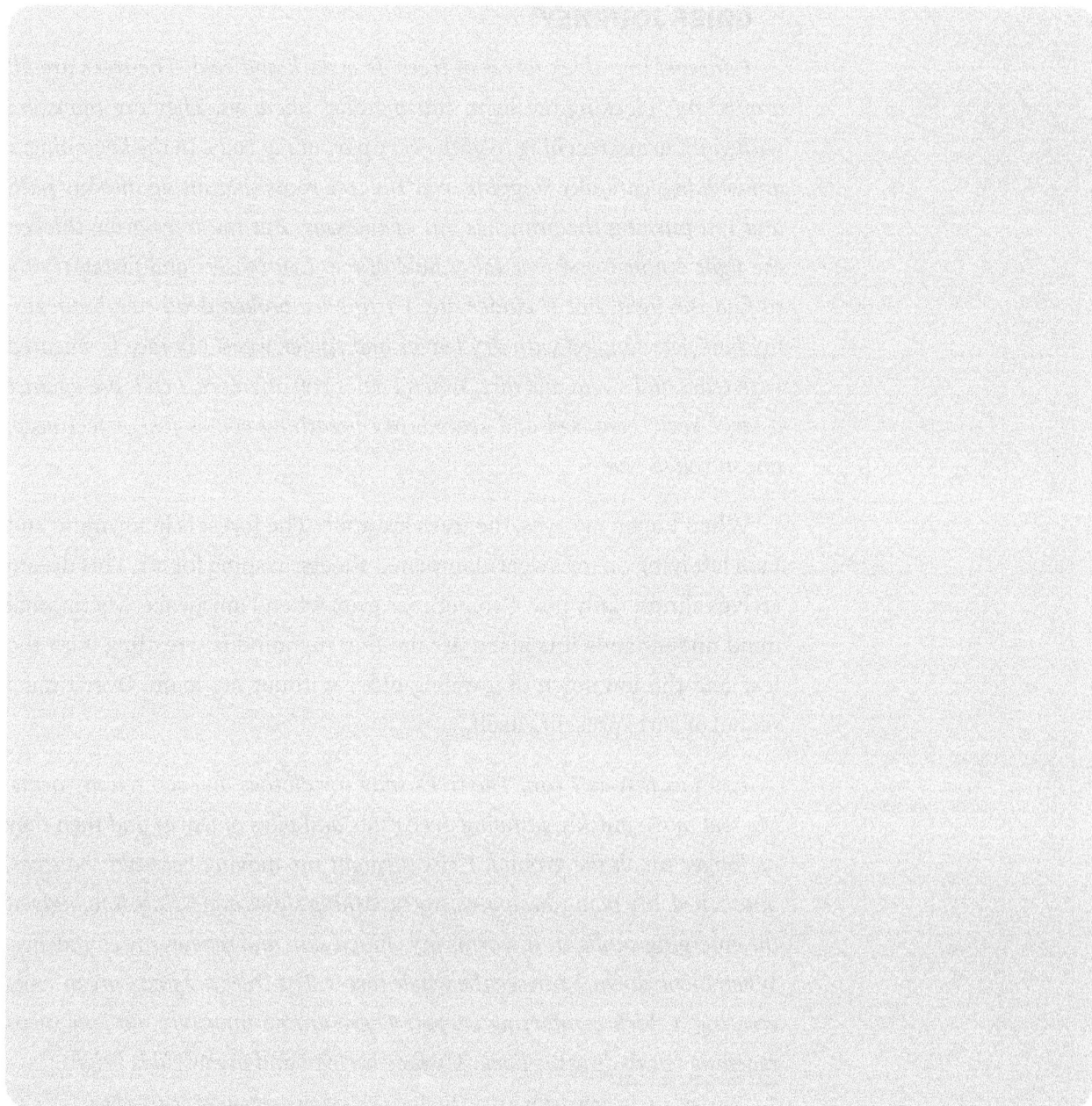

GRIEF JOURNEY[3]

I am lost in a thick forest of trees. It is dark and cold. The trees are all around me, blocking the light, causing dark shadows. They are monsters with giant arms, reaching to grab every part of my body. In the beginning, I am walking, carefully stepping over the tree roots that jut up into my path and I'm pushing the branches out of the way. But the trees grow thicker, the light dimmer and fear takes hold of me. I run faster and faster, trying to find the light, but it eludes me. I trip over broken dead tree branches; my hair gets tangled with dry leaves and spider webs. My face is smeared with tears and sweat and dirt. When I can't run anymore, I collapse against a large rock, confused and scared. My breathing comes fast. I feel deep, uncontrolled panic.

When I open my eyes, the trees are gone. The forest is in my mind and I am left lying on my sweat-dampened sheets, gasping for air. This dream arrives almost daily now—sometimes even when I am awake. My rational mind understands it is just a dream; that my mind is wrestling with the fear and the unknown of growing older without my mom. Over time a sequel of sorts presents itself.

I run as fast as I can. The trees snag my clothes and scratch my arms. My feet move quickly, jumping over roots and piles of leaves and then they no longer touch the ground. I rise straight up, moving between the trees, untouched. My panic dissipates, my breathing slows and I stare longingly at the emerging sunlight. It warms my chilled skin and renews my confidence. When I look down, I can see the whole forest. The trees are fuzzy green spots creating a thick comforting carpet. There are no monsters, no long arms reaching out to drag me back. My face is clean and my world is bright.

---

3   Dreams are an important part of healing. This is an example of one of mine.

This new dream becomes my mantra; this forest, my source for healing. I realized eventually when my grief was too great and my resources too low, I became trapped in the forest, unable to see the light, unable to see the forest for what it was. But over time I am capable of walking calmly through my forest, no longer scared of the unseen, fully aware that I will emerge from it. I actively visualize this new mantra whenever I can. I walk the forest so many times I make a wide path, flattening the leaves and crawling vines. Soon my path has a distinct entrance and exit. Soon I am able to turn around and look back at the forest. Soon I am able to remember what the forest is and why I have to travel there, why it is so important to come out the other side. I come to understand the forest is my memories, my grief, my feelings of lost opportunity and deep sadness. The journey through the forest is my healing path.

"Do not go where the path may lead, go instead where there is no path, and leave a trail."

~ Ralph Waldo Emerson

Write down your dreams. They may be comforting or strange or confusing. No matter what, jot them down and explore what they mean to you.

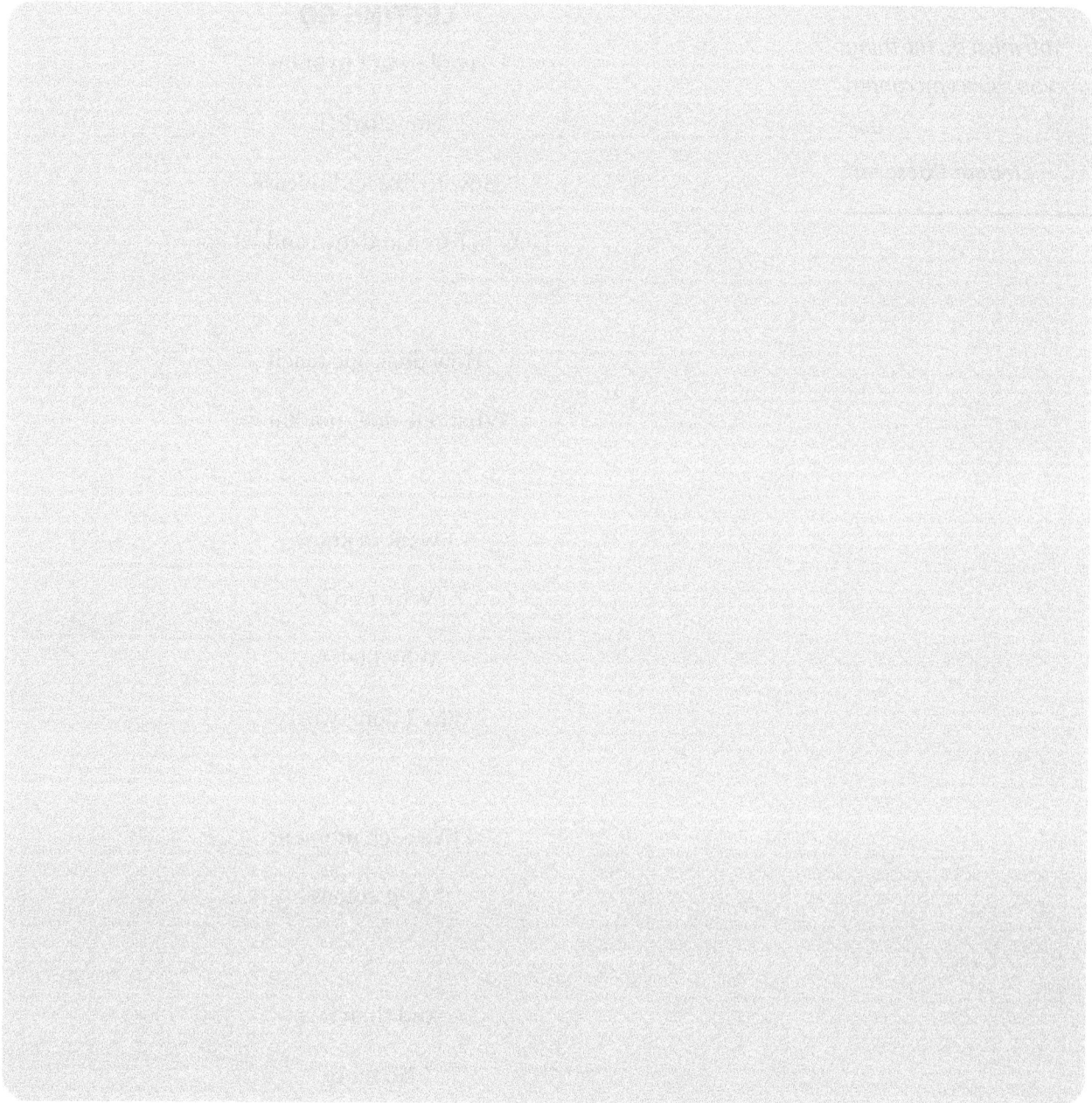

"You must do the thing you think you cannot do."

~ Eleanor Roosevelt

LETTING GO

People want to know

How to do it

How to live and release

How to listen and love and let go

How does one teach

What one does not know

I want to know

Why I do it

Why I let go

Why I don't worry

I live each moment

As it comes

And then it is

No more

What must you let go of in order to heal?

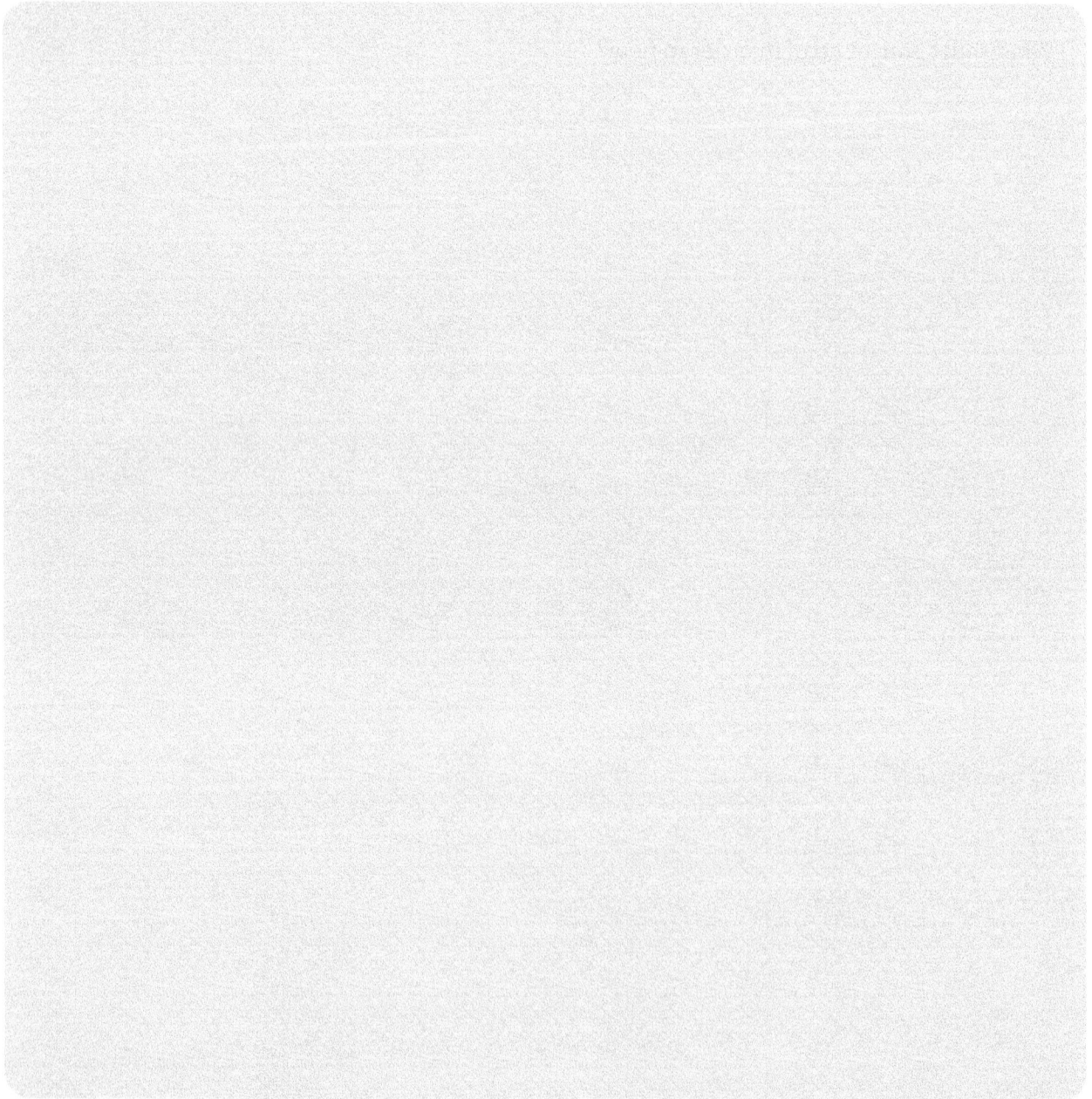

SURVIVAL SKILLS

Smile every day

Never go to bed angry

Play hard, work hard

Love is forever

Know yourself

Respect yourself

Love yourself

Love the world more

Be grateful

For what you have

Be thankful

For your health

Live honestly

Stay positive

Laugh daily

Be content

"I cried at first . . . and then, it was such a beautiful day, that I forgot to be unhappy."
~ Frances Noyes Hart

What lessons have you learned from your loved one? How did they impact your life?

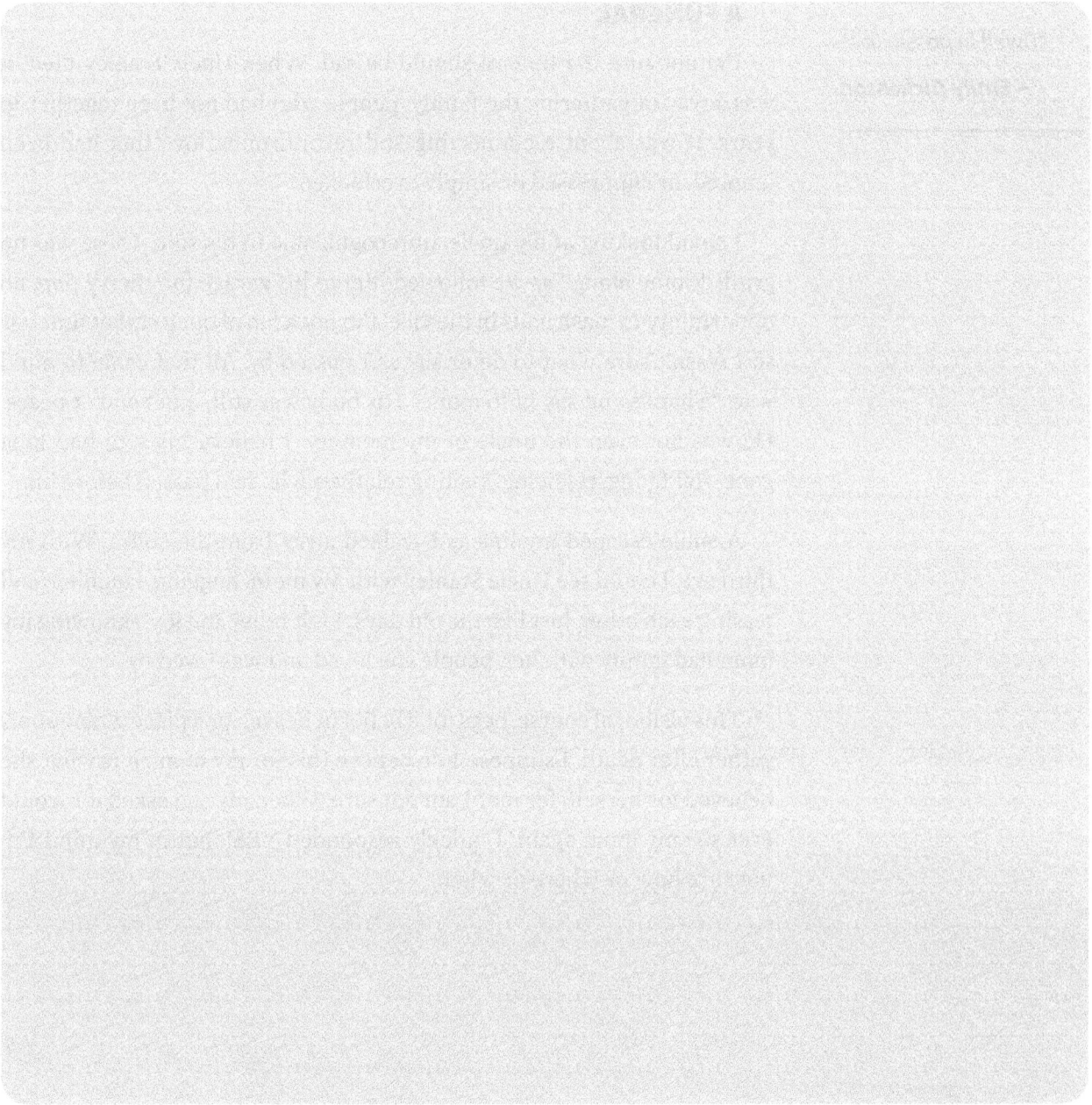

"Dwell in possibility."

~ Emily Dickenson

A FUNERAL

I'm not sure if a funeral should be sad. When Uncle Stanley died, it was a way of gathering the family; people who had not been together in years. It was about reconnecting and reconfirming love that had been ignored, or suppressed or simply overlooked.

I stood looking at my uncle, unrecognizable in his suit; There was no gruff, "Come along" as we followed him to his garage for cherry pop, no opportunity to mash nails in the vice. I'm not a fan of open casket funerals so I wasn't sure what to do or say as I passed by. All that came to mind was, "Thanks and say hi to mom." His body was still, quiet and at peace. He was not even the uncle of my memory. I believe his soul had long gone—off flying, rejoicing, visiting relatives who had passed before him.

A smile escaped my lips as I walked away from the coffin. With my third eye, I could see Uncle Stanley with my mom: hugging, laughing, and teasing each other, just like the old days. I felt relief and joy—knowing my mom had family with her, people she loved and was loved by.

This vision, of course, begs for a belief in heaven or a place where souls gather after death. I suppose I do believe this for my mom, it is what she believed for herself, for me? I am not sure. When my son asked if I would ever see my mom again, I quickly responded YES!; but in my mind I'm not sure how or where or when.

There is always sadness from the loss of someone we love. But as we move towards acceptance we are better able to appreciate and celebrate the relationship with less distress. What can you celebrate today?

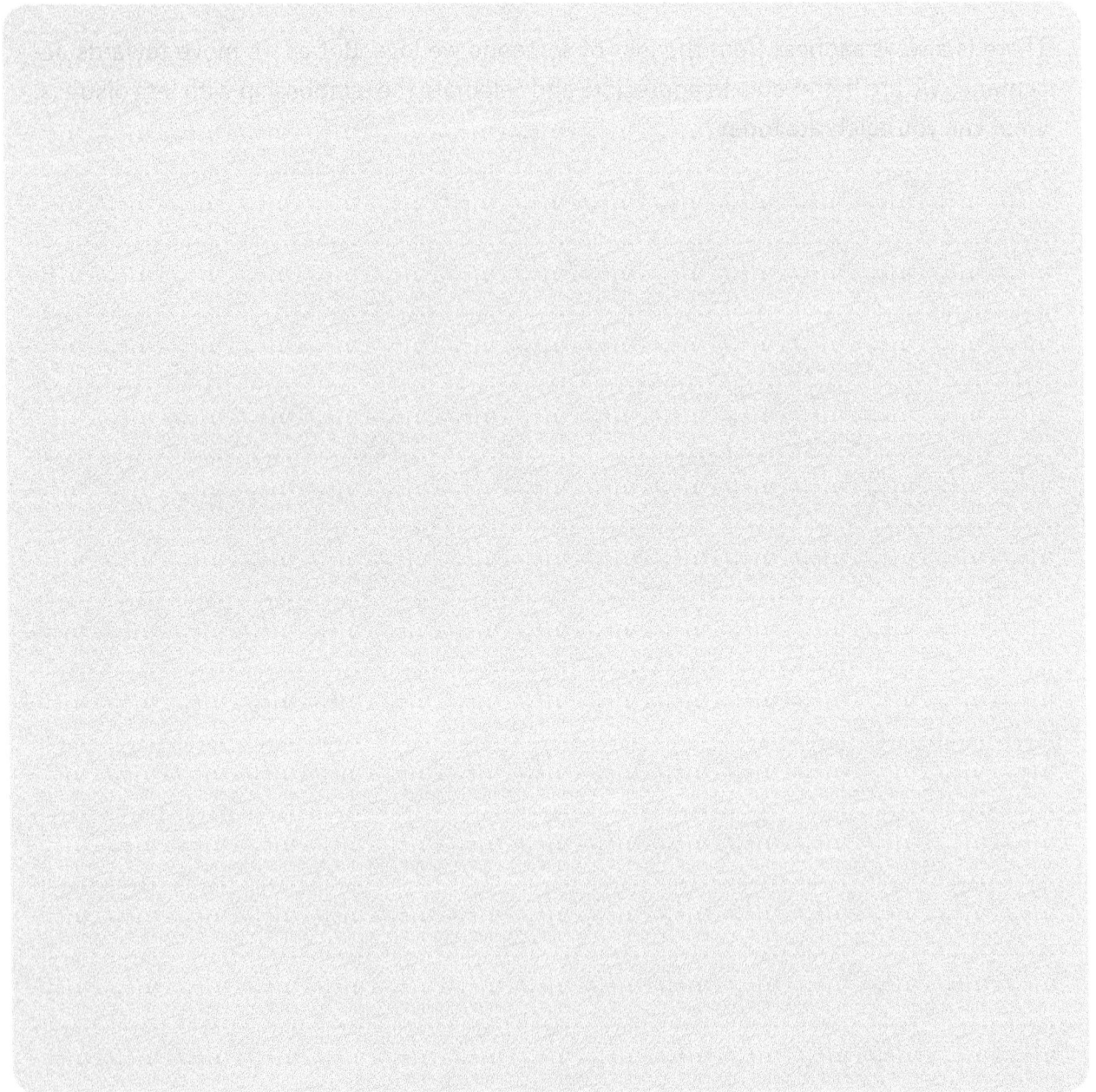

GOOD NIGHT WHISPER

Dear Mom,

How'd you do it—watch me grow up? Did you have regrets, did you sneak into my room at night and watch me sleep; the way I do with my boys? At night, when it's dark and the house is quiet, I like to watch them sleep. I kiss my eldest upon the head and run my fingers through his soft brown hair; he rolls over, stretches and releases a slow, low moan. God, I love that sound. I fix his covers and breathe deeply before turning to his brother in the next bed. He lays there half-covered and I catch a glimpse of myself: always having one foot sticking out the side of the covers for fresh air. I kiss his cheek; he stirs, grits his teeth and exhales. After he finishes repositioning himself, I fix his covers and again exhale contentedly.

They have grown so fast. By day I cannot wait for them to grow up, but at night I dare to wish they'll never change. They are my past, my future and my present, all rolled into one. How do I capture that feeling I get when we reach for each other's hands as we cross the street how those tiny fingers curl against my palm? How did you do it? Whisper the secrets to me while I sleep.

Good night.

There will always be daily reminders of your loved one—moments that make you laugh out loud or collapse in tears. Take a few moments and jot down those memories. How might you hold onto the happy ones and begin to release the ones that keep you stuck?

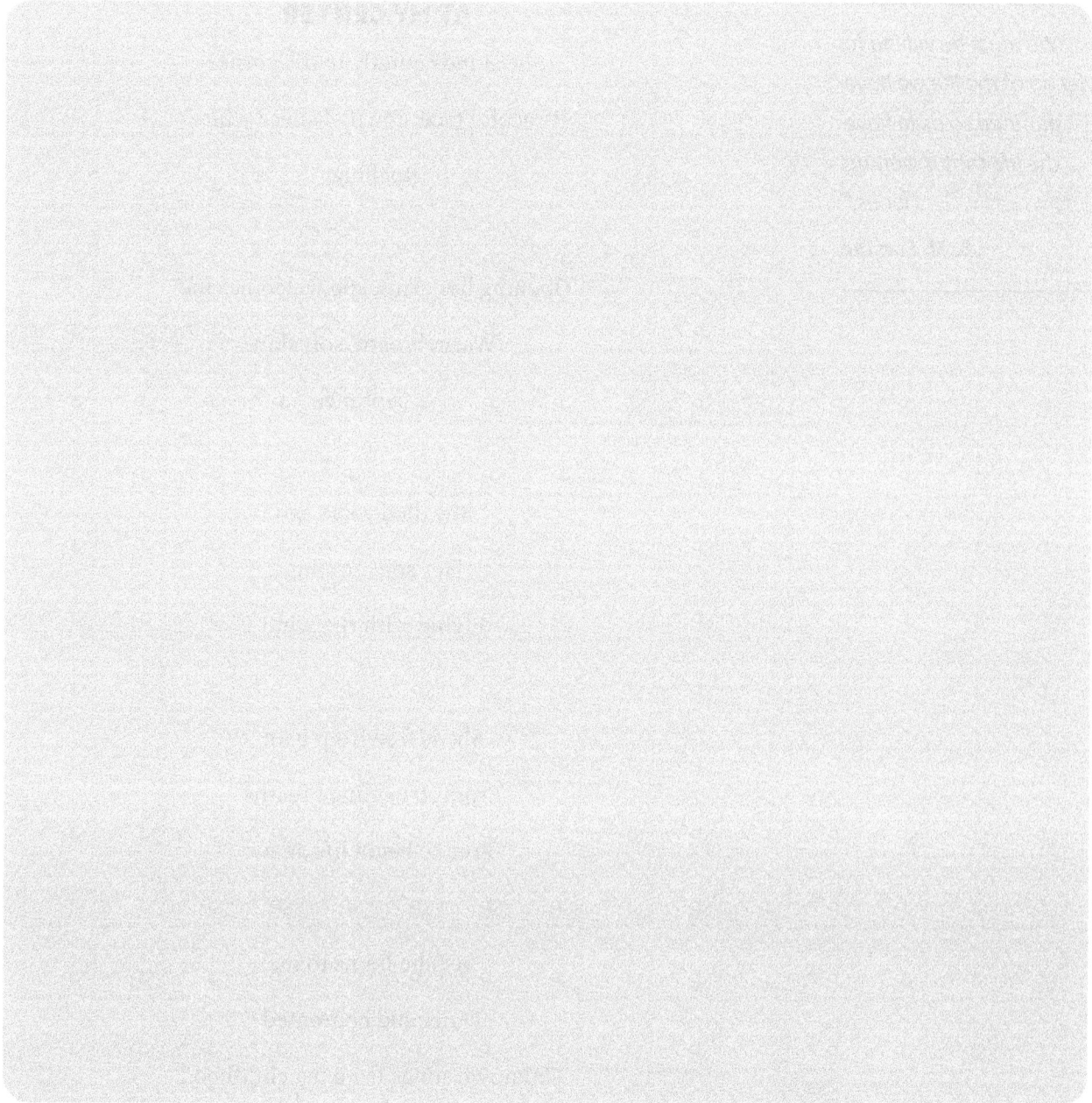

"We must be willing to let go of the life we have planned so as to have the life that is waiting for us."

~ E. M. Forster

AT MY CENTER

She stands quietly in the corner

Peaceful face, gown of sheer white

Rocking

Opening her arms, she welcomes me

Warm breath, soft skin

Acceptance

She died years ago

Her soul circling

Flying with the wind

She is free from pain

From struggling breaths

Free to begin life anew

Yet she hums to me

Quiet and contented

Unknown songs from my childhood

There comes a time when we fully realize and accept our loss. In order for you to come to this place, what must you embrace? What must you let go of?

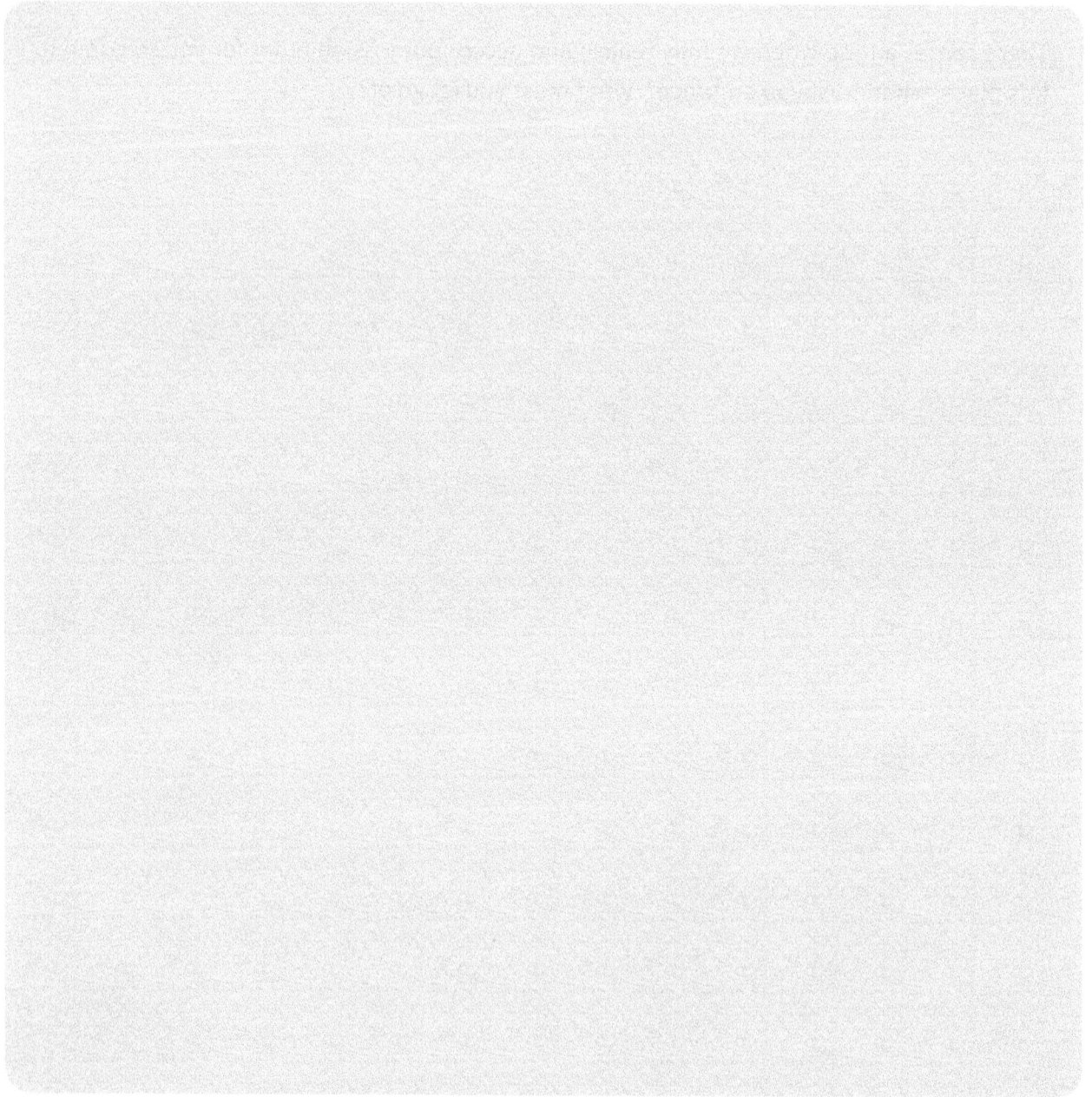

TRUSTING MYSELF

For many years I have found it difficult to really *look* at myself because what was reflected back was Mom. When I looked at my hands, I saw her hands, when I read my handwriting, I saw hers, and when I glimpsed myself in the mirror, it was her face looking back at me. We looked too much alike to deny the connection and for a time I lost myself. But the demands of my own children and my personal need for closure have slowly pushed me forward until once again it is my face staring back from the mirror and Mom has moved from my head to my heart.

I don't have the answers to the unending questions about raising children, dealing with household finances and dealing with my feelings of inadequacy. I want so badly to dial her number and hear her calming, reassuring voice refocus my scattered mind, but she's not there. So I turn to the window and wait if I am patient the voice will come, the answer will present itself and I am left grateful. Her voice has become my inner guide; her knowledge, my knowledge. If only I will be still, ask the question and listen.

"As with all life changes, at some point you have to own who and what you are. You have to accept it so that you can move forward and become who you are meant to be."

~ Catherine Tidd
Confessions of a Mediocre Widow

An essential part of healing is trusting that we'll be okay despite our loss. Write down what your loved one would say to help you trust that you will heal. What messages are they sharing?

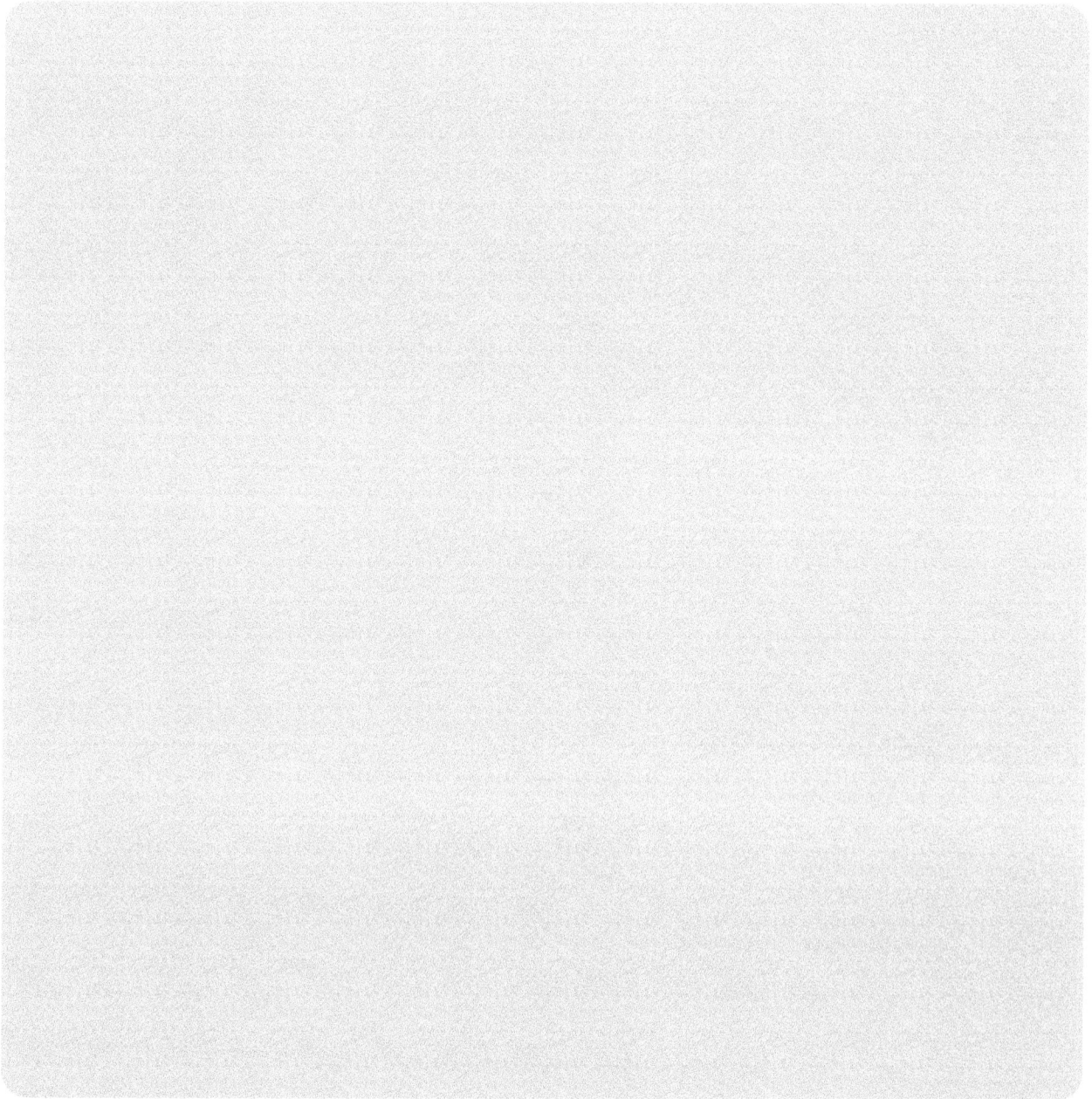

Phase 4: Memory

...reminiscence, remembrance, recollection...

Here we make our home, for in memory our loved one lives. All lives are filled with good and bad experiences, highs and lows. In *Memory* we get to choose the memories we want to collect. We get to choose their impact; holding close those which empower and releasing those which enrage.

You will return here often and over time fill the remainder of this book with stories and life lessons. Here you will heal from the inside out accepting the loss and accepting yourself in a new place.

Remember – Savor – Learn – Renew.

"The highest tribute to the dead is not grief, but gratitude."
- Thornton Wilder

Make a list of memories here, things that fill your head: scenes, smells, visions, dreams. Just jot down what comes to mind, revisiting this list as new memories surface.

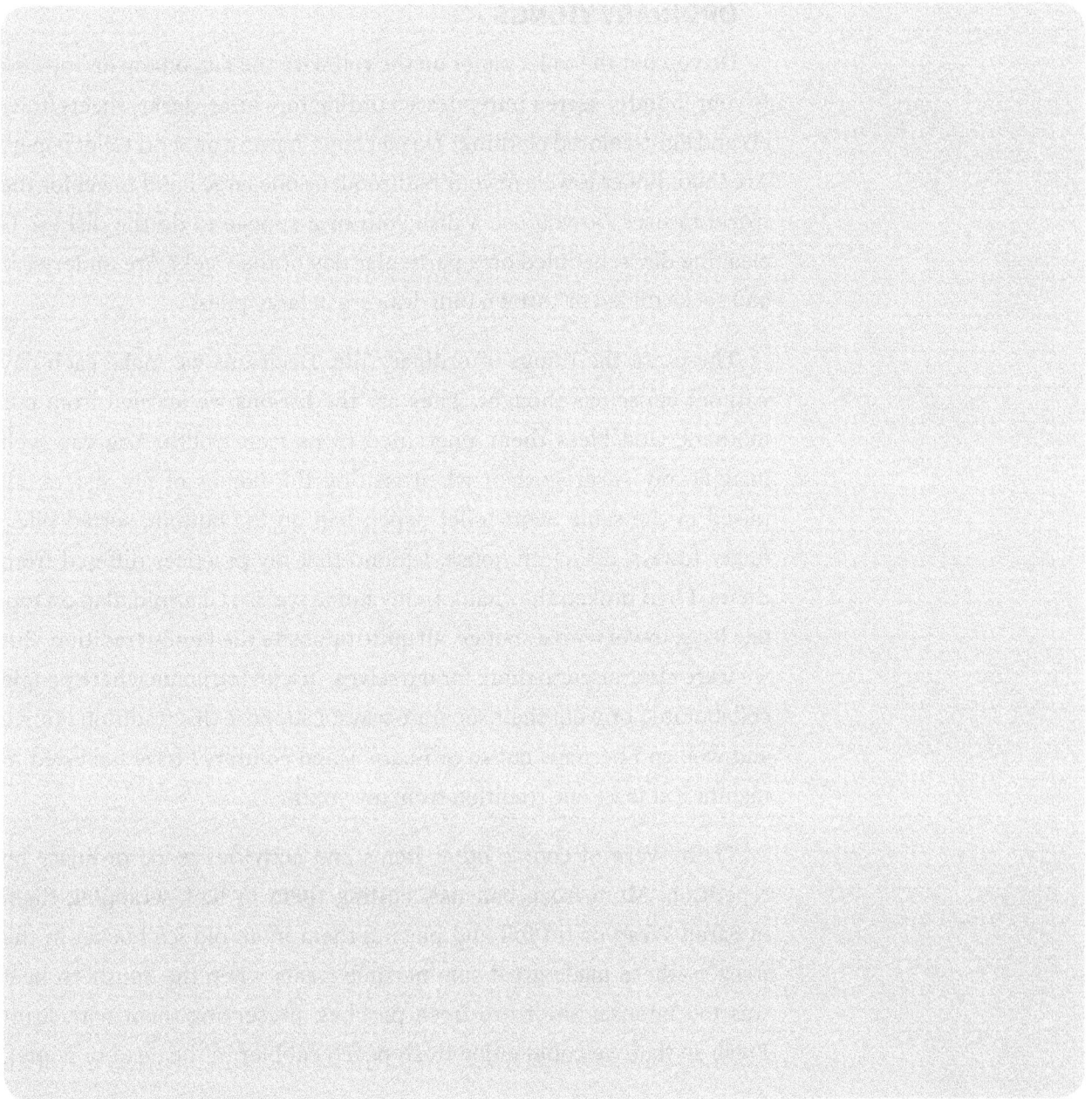

ORDINARY THINGS

Do you put the toilet paper on the roll with the flap on top or bottom? Is your laundry sorted into piles according to whites, darks, sheets/towels and light-colored clothing? Do you buy Charmin or Scott toilet paper? Are there finger towels in your bathroom or one large hand towel for the world to use? Do you use a dishcloth or a sponge to do the dishes? Is cleaning day scheduled on a particular day of the week? Are underwear and socks folded or thrown into drawers in large piles?

These are the things of ordinary life. Decisions we make each day without conscious thought. They are the lessons we learned from our mothers, God bless them, engrained in us from youth. You can well imagine my surprise then when visiting the homes of my sisters, all raised in the same Scott toilet paper, flap on the bottom, sorted piles, finger towels, dishcloth house. I found that my practices differed from theirs. I had broken the chain. In my home we use Charmin, flap on top, one large towel with a sponge, all quite opposite the family tradition. But we were also raised to think for ourselves, in a loving home where people collaborated or went their separate ways. I suppose this tradition is alive and well and perhaps not so ordinary. I find comfort I have managed to maintain at least one tradition from my youth.

There were of course other items and activities made ordinary by repetition. Mom froze bananas, cutting them in half, wrapping them in Saran Wrap or tin foil and placing them in an old ice bucket in the freezer—these made great summertime treats when the Southern heat was too intense. She froze fresh peaches, preserving them with Fruit Fresh so that we could enjoy fresh peach cobbler in the dead of winter.

Mom also invented the original frozen yogurt by placing pre-stirred Dannon (which was about to expire) into the freezer. It tasted great, took a long time to eat and we thought it was a treat! What a woman. As a mother myself now, I realize she was being creative with healthy food, but as a child I took for granted the ordinary offerings of her kitchen.

After playing kickball in the backyard with the neighborhood kids, that frozen banana tasted especially sweet. It had a way of cooling me off while satisfying the dull growl in my stomach. We always had a group of kids at our house and mom always had enough bananas to go around. In my youthful ignorance I believed my experience to be plain and ordinary. Surely every family gathered for dinner each night; every family discussed daily activities and ate chicken, rice and salad in some variation four days a week. In my mind we were an ordinary, average family of five, living a middle class life in a middle class neighborhood. But, as I grew older I realized what I experienced at home was *not* the norm of the neighborhood. My life was made special by my mom's every day activities.

"I know artists whose medium is life itself, and who express the inexpressible without brush, pencil, chisel or guitar. They neither paint, nor dance. Their medium is Being. Whatever their hand touches has increased Life. They see and don't have to draw. They are the artists of being alive."

~ Frederick Franck

Often we take for granted those ordinary things of life that with reflection become extra-or-dinary. What extra-ordinary things do you notice? How have they enhanced your life? How might you carry them forward?

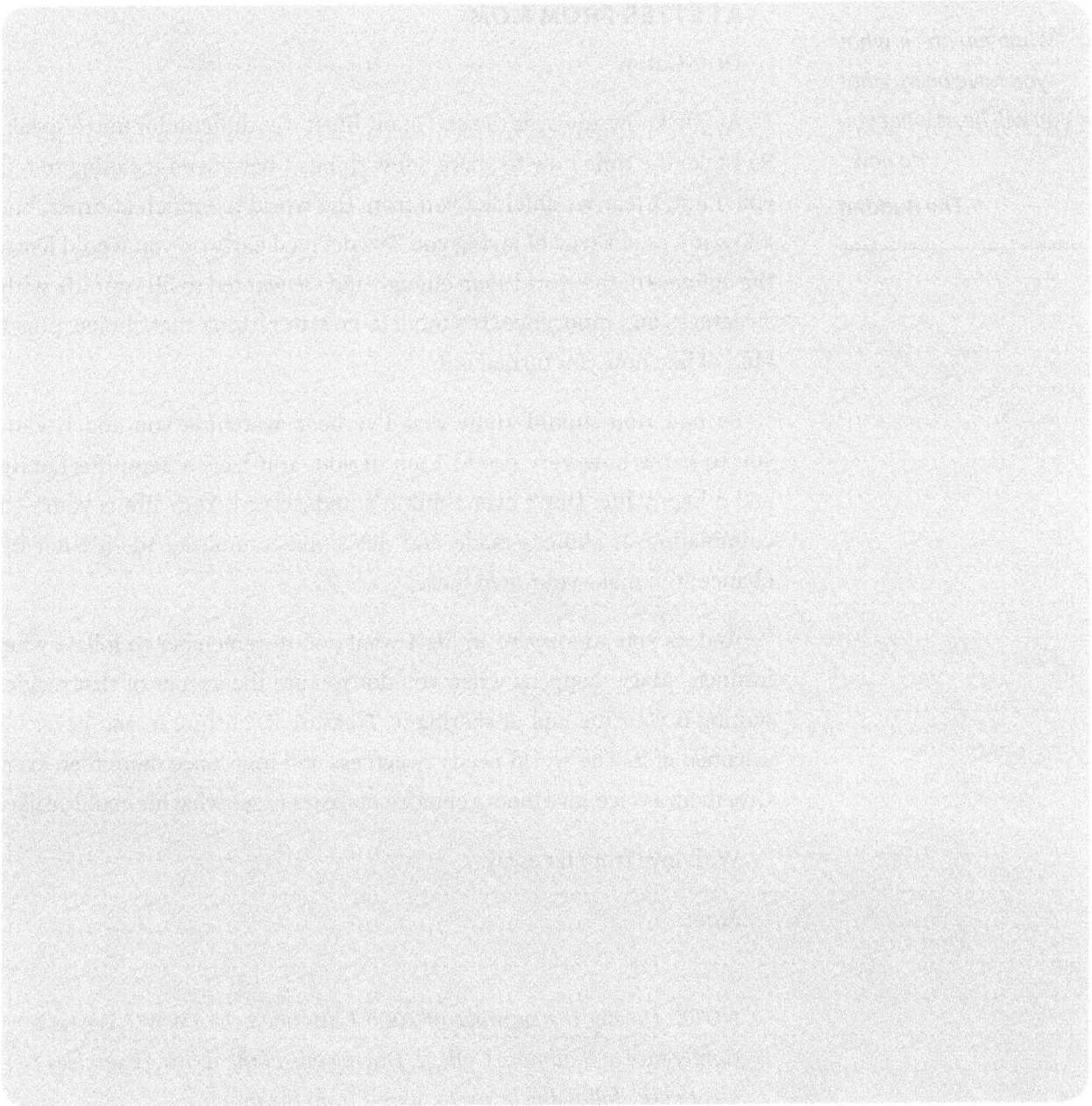

> *"What you are, is what you have been, what you will be, is what you do now."*
>
> **~ The Buddha**

A LETTER FROM *MOM*

Dear Cathy,

As you know, towards the end of my life it was difficult for me to speak. So I take the time now to share a few things I have been meaning to tell you. First, I fear we shielded you from the world too much at times, but know it was our way of loving you. We decided early on you would learn the ugliness of the world soon enough and we wanted to fill your life with sweetness and innocence. It's too late now to rethink that choice, plus I kind of like how you turned out.

Second, you should know that I've been watching you and I want you to know how very proud I am of you. You have a beautiful family and a happy life. Don't ever think it's undeserved. Your life is yours—a culmination of choices made and decisions committed to—it's not by chance. You make your own luck.

And, as you go forward in life I want you to remember to follow your instincts. Magic happens when you do. You are the keeper of that magic: writing is your method of sharing it. Treasure it, nurture it, and never be ashamed of it. The world needs sweetness and innocence more than ever. Give them a voice, give them a choice—make them see what life could be like.

With love from far away,

Mom

NOTE: During the summer of 2006 I attended the IWWG Writer's Conference at Skidmore College. During one of the writing exercises I created the following letter to myself from my mom.

Search your soul. What words of wisdom does your loved one wish to impart? What do you need to hear?

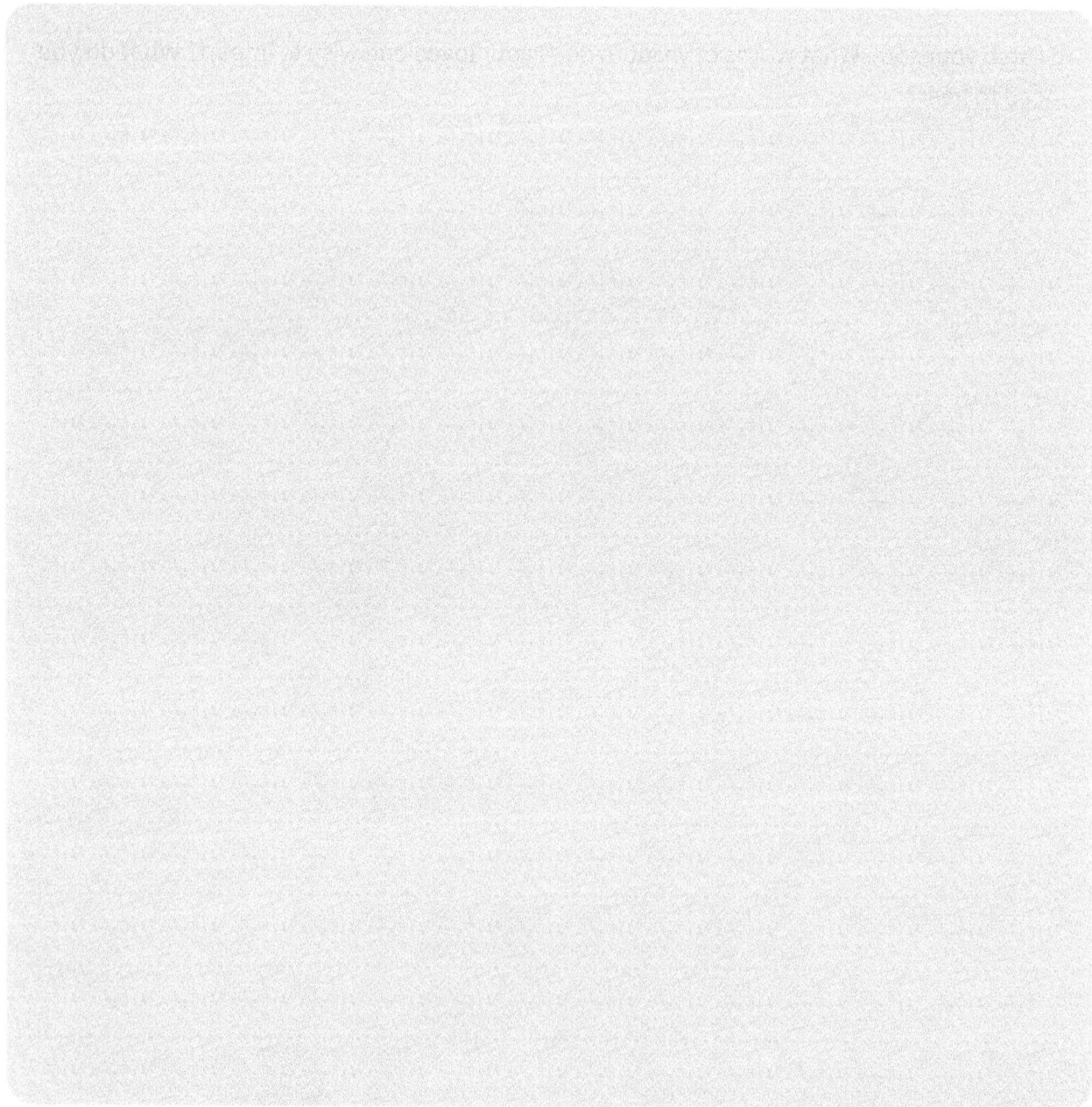

GHOST BEHIND MY EYELIDS

I recently started exercising at 5:30am. Call me crazy but there is something humbling and inspiring about the pre-dawn hour. When I return home the sky is still dark and the house is still. The only sounds are the fan on the furnace and the scratching of my pen across the paper. In the shadows, I can feel you—I know you are there, watching me, smiling your all-knowing smile. I can feel your pride from the other side and it warms me. I try each day to remember you, to emulate you. It gives me strength. I am thankful for your guidance and grateful for your example. Even after death, you continue to teach me, the methods have changed, but the result is the same.

Putting pencil to paper I try to describe you, that ghost I see behind my eyelids, resting in the shadow, listening to my heartbeat, smiling at my thoughts. How can I explain the you I feel in my life every day? Will anyone understand the presence I feel? Can anyone acknowledge it? See it? Feel it? Sometimes I doubt. I think, "How could this be? How could you be there? How could I feel you? Surely it's just my imagination; surely it's just my desire." Yet the sensation brings me comfort, so why fight it, why question—just relax and enjoy and allow whatever it is to fill the void, even if the shadows disappear in the light of day.

"After winter comes the summer. After night comes the dawn. And after every storm, there comes clear, open skies."

~ Samuel Rutherford

While it's not always the case, many people have unexplained moments when their loved ones can be felt or seen. Have you had this experience? What was it like?

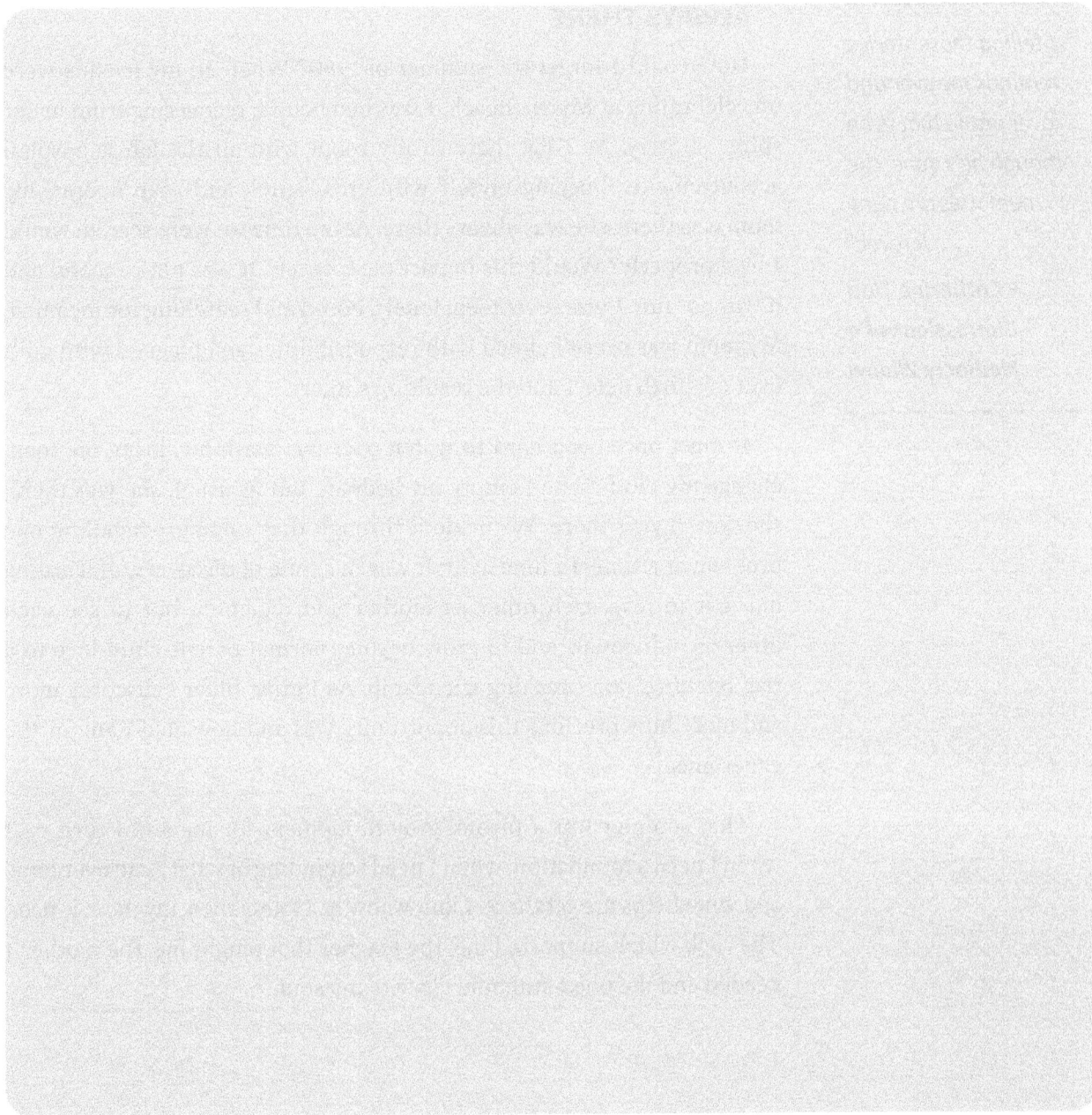

> *"…telling those stories reminds me over and over again that even though he's gone, the memories are mine forever."*
>
> *~ Catherine Tidd*
> ***Confessions of a Mediocre Widow***

ALWAYS THERE

How could I forget the summer of 1980? When all my friends were off celebrating at Myrtle Beach, I was bed bound, recovering from major spinal surgery. As I lay there in my room with all the latest hospital accoutrements, busying myself with cross-stitch and soap operas, my mom was there, she was always there. At the time we were scared: would I heal properly? Would this impact me forever? It was not peaceful and it was not fun. I was seventeen; lonely, bored and searching for meaning. My mom was overwhelmed with responsibilities and plagued with guilt over my birth defect and the resulting surgery.

It must have been hard to watch over me: wash me, bring me food, change my clothes, and empty my bedpan. But as usual, she was there; she was always there. We made it through that summer—handling one problem at a time. In hindsight, it was our time of discovery, of learning not just to love each other as mother and daughter, but to see each other as individuals and to grow beyond normal parent-child love to a real bonding, non-breaking friendship. As I grow older I discover more and more how precious this opportunity was and how glad I am for the experience.

That summer was a pivotal growth moment for me and I turn to it when I need a foundation, when I need reminding of what I can overcome and what helps me get there. I know now as I knew then, my mom is near. The rock which supported me, the teacher that taught me, the mother I needed and the one I still hold close to my soul.

Look back at the list you made at the beginning of this chapter. Pick a few meaningful memories to write about here.

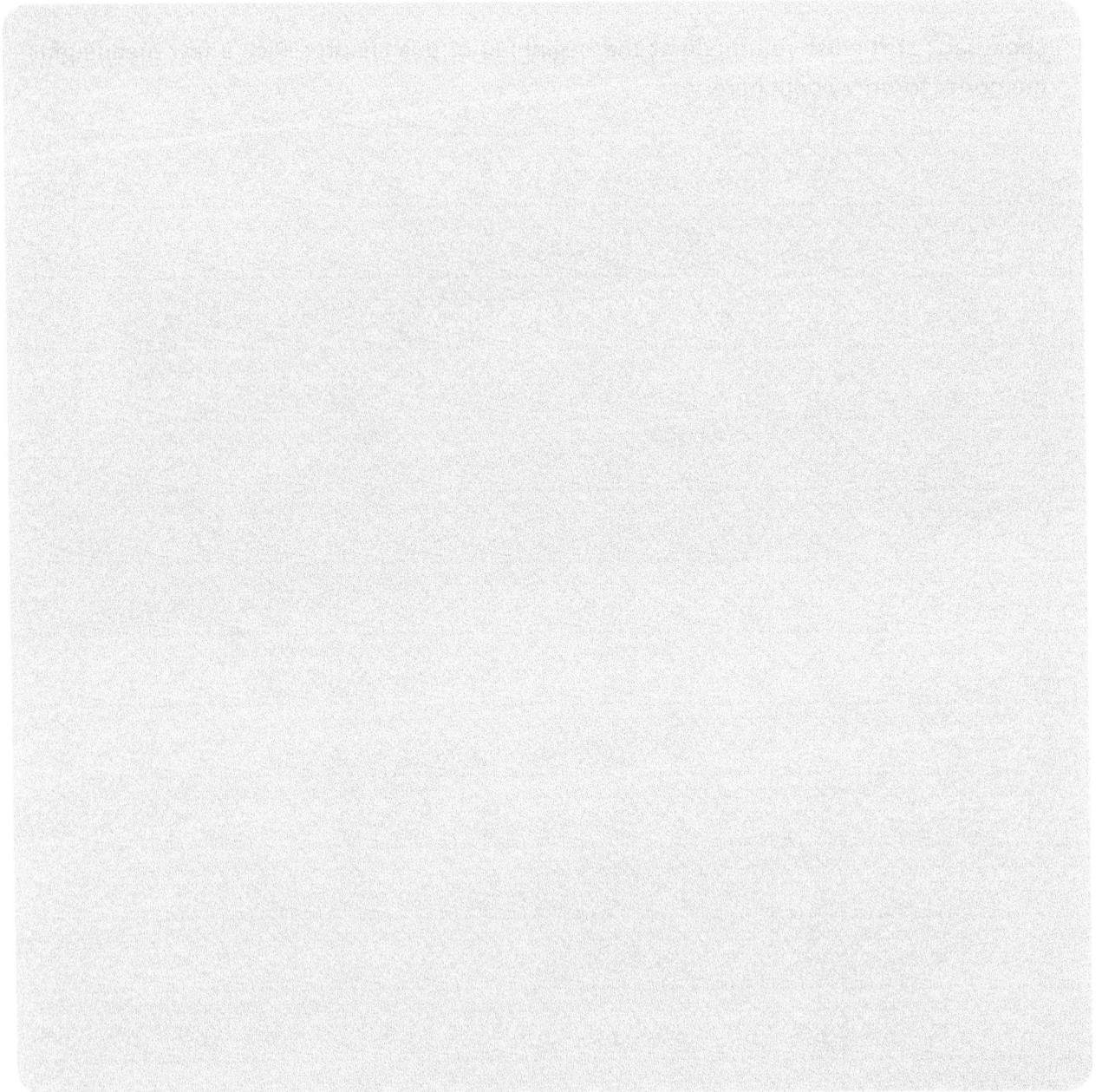

HER GIFT

Sunshine in blue, cloudless skies

Yellow light streams through blinds and I

Sit anxiously

Legs tucked under.

Eggs bump in boiling water

Smiles, chatter, cups and color

White vinegar

And wire spoon.

Colored disks pop and fizzle

Dark spots of rainbow sizzle

Upon my knees

Impatient stir.

Her face smiles with love and light

Laughter fills the space and I

Hold my breath

My eyes squeezed tight.

"What lies behind us and what lies before us are tiny matters compared to what lies within us."

~ Oliver Wendell Holmes

Beeps of time awaken me

Eager faces look to see

Magic colors

And she appears.

Thru dust motes suspended in sunlight

She smiles and fills up our place

With love and warmth

Approving gaze.

I breathe in her warmth and light

Little hands dance with delight

A second look

A whisper and

Gone

Yet forever there.

What gifts were you given? What lies within you as a result of knowing this person?

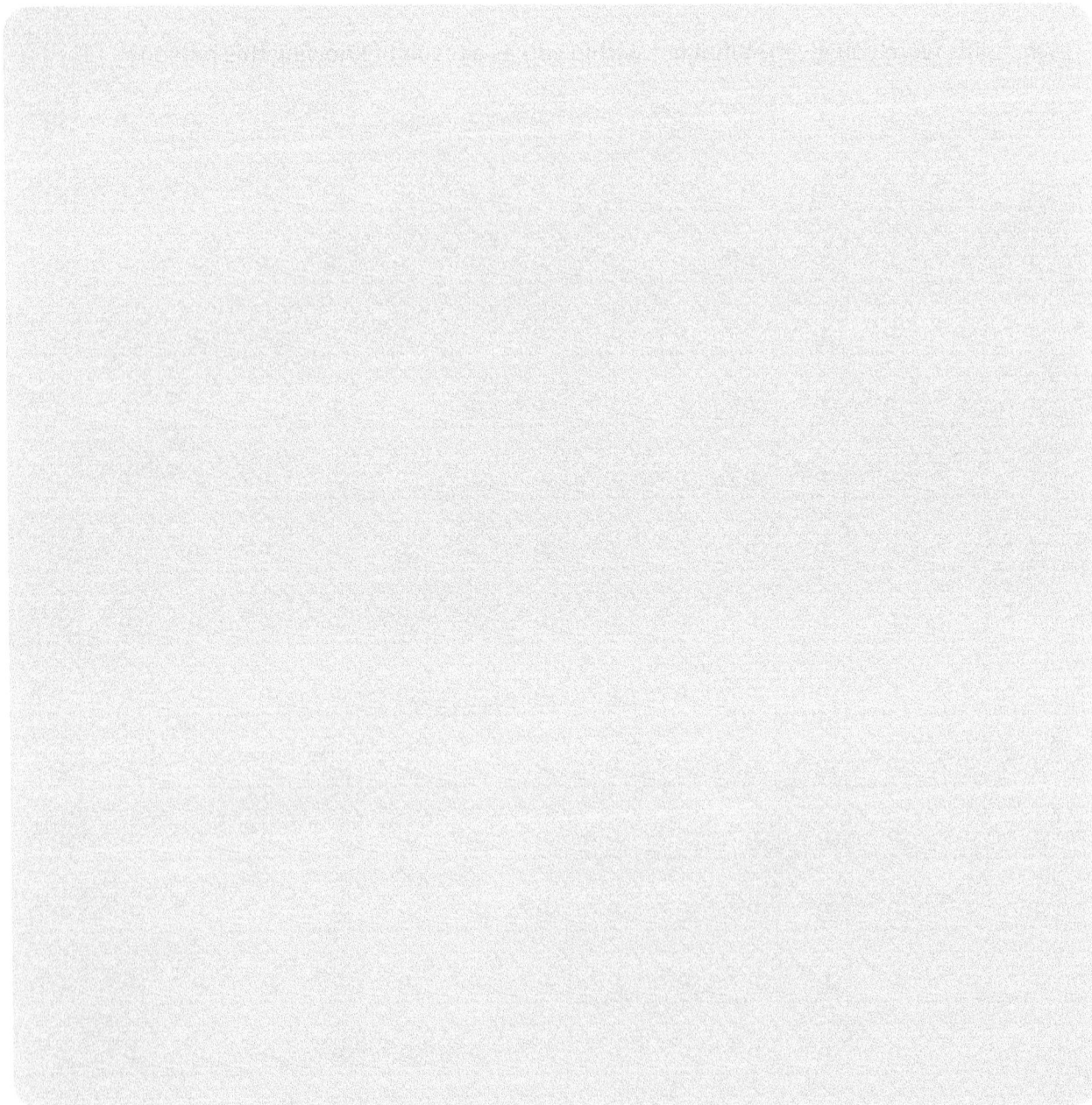

IT'S NOT THE HAT

While shopping for back-to-school clothes at Target, I watched my young sons run around the Boys Department looking at shirts and shorts, pajamas and sweatshirts. Eventually they came around to the new assortment of hats and belts. They were busy trying on all the hats when I started laughing. "What's so funny?" they inquired. I smiled a big smile and exclaimed, "It's not the hat, it's how you wear it." They didn't quite get it, but laughed anyway.

As they continued their fun, I laughed to myself and nodded to the world, acknowledging my mother's wisdom. I remember the day so clearly. I was in high school and we were shopping for a new Easter outfit. The clothes in the Young Miss department were coordinated with matching hats. As my mother lifted one from the rack I sadly announced, "I don't look good in hats. I can't possibly wear that." Mom just giggled, winked and replied, "It's not really the hat, it's how you wear it!" Mom turned to the mirror, tilted her head slightly to the right and gently placed the wide-brimmed hat on her head. She turned to me quite pleased with herself, the hat sitting slightly askew. "Perfect!" she announced.

It wasn't until years later that I really understood the underlying wisdom she shared with me that day. I was having a hard time with some teammates at work. I was upset and concerned about their negative approach to our project. I needed a way to demonstrate how important commitment and desire to make a difference was to our success. I needed a story to share to make my message sink in—attitude is a choice. My mother's words came drifting back to me. As they did, it suddenly occurred to me the hat could be anything. It could be a piece of clothing, a behavior, even an attitude. I shared the story and encouraged conversation about how the moral of the story might apply to the work at hand. I walked out of that meeting smiling to myself and relishing my mom's infinite wisdom.

What examples did your loved one set for you and others? What lessons did they impart?

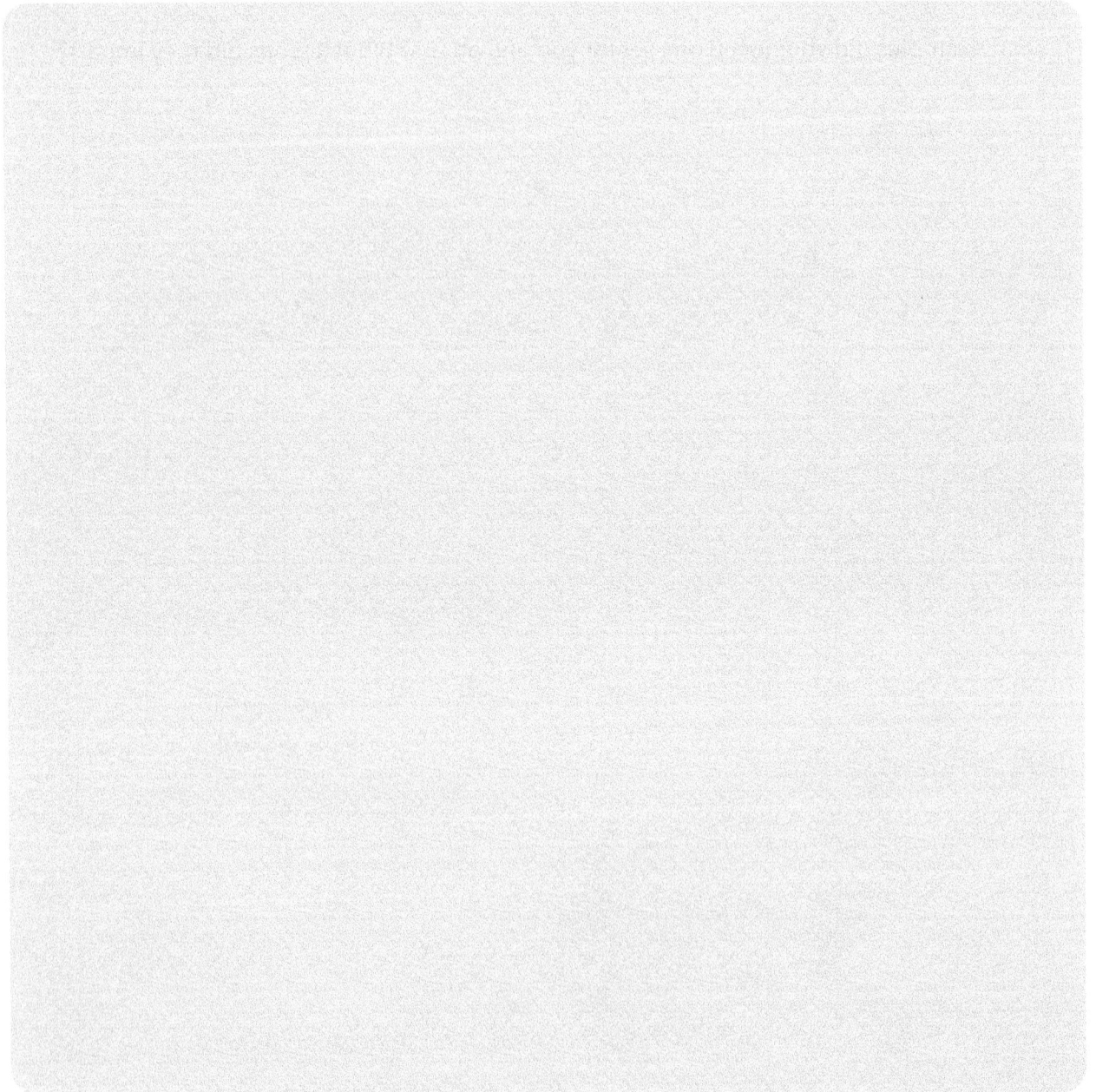

MONKEY FACES

It's September now and Home Depot has pansies on sale. Their little monkey faces smile at me as I enter. But I walk by, concentrating on the required plumbing supplies. As I fill my basket with pipes and plugs, I hear them. Their whispers are soft and faint, their words, some nonsense verse. As I pass them a second time, they stand a little straighter, forcing their wide faces skyward. The whisper becomes clearer and more distinct—

We will brighten your garden

We will shine through the rain

We will rest in the snow

And return with the spring

Her spirit will tend us

Tears of joy will feed us

Sunshine and moonlight

Our day's contentment

The whisper becomes a chant, keeping pace with my heart. It is familiar and comforting. For several moments I stand and listen. I close my eyes and breathe them in. I will not resist them for they touch that place deep in my soul, they soothe the pain, and fill the void.

> *"Let us be grateful to people who make us happy; they are the gardeners who make our souls blossom."*
>
> *~ Marcel Proust*

Now they sit on my front porch, their eager monkey faces wait patiently. They wait for my hands to till the soil, for that long drink of cool water, for the comfort of the earth. They wait for her blessing.

Symbols, like the pansies in this story, can be powerful tools for holding onto positive memories. What do you associate with your loved one? How can you keep that positive memory active in your life?

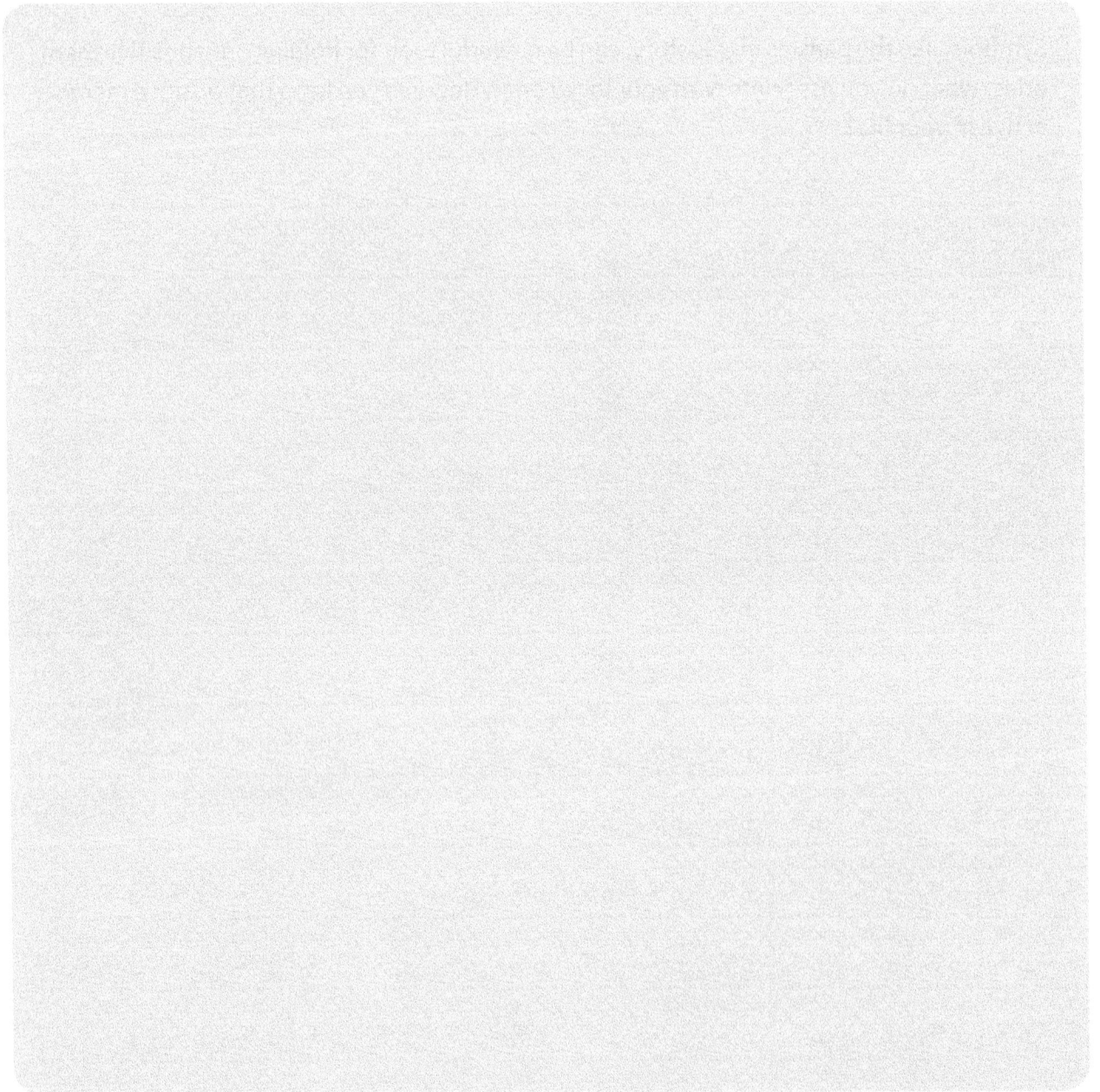

EPILOGUE

I am 54 years old—only a few years shy of the time of life when my mother was first diagnosed. I do think about it and try daily to live my life with intention—recognizing how precious each day is and working hard to leave it better today than yesterday. This is yet another lesson my mother taught me.

It has been 17 years since Mom's passing and I still miss her every day. Her picture still sits in my office, her face occasionally shows up in my mirror, I still cry during certain commercials when they bring forward a lost memory or lingering regret, and I talk to her when there are things to share or questions to be answered. I am happy and my life is sweet. My kids are young men now with no real memory of their grandmother, but they know the stories, they laugh with me and hug me when I need it. My husband of twenty-five years understands—he doesn't judge or try to make me feel better. He just acknowledges and reassures and is always there when I need him.

I know my sisters live in a similar space—balancing current reality with past memory. They have moved forward at their own pace, in their own way as each of you have. It is important for that to be okay. My dad remarried in 2012. I think it was most difficult for him to move forward but once he was past the grief and the guilt I think he was able to acknowledge the need to share his life. It was an important step and we are enriched by the addition to the family.

Please use the remainder of this book to capture your feelings, thoughts and stories. Use this space to vent and ask questions.

Use this space to heal.

Epilogue

Epilogue

Epilogue

Epilogue

Epilogue

Epilogue

Epilogue

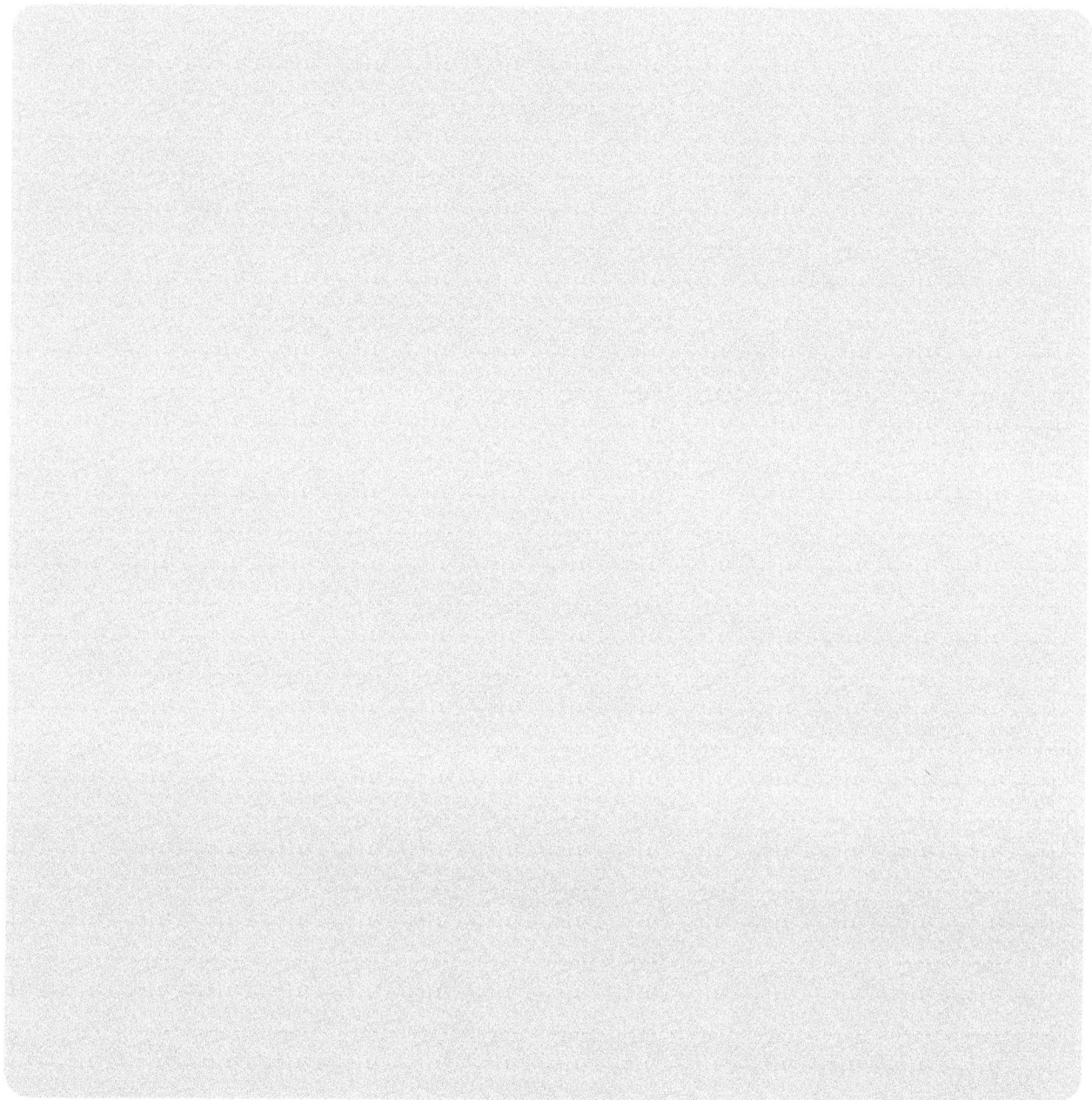

Lightning Source UK Ltd.
Milton Keynes UK
UKHW03f1830290818
328005UK00004B/227/P

9 781628 654103